Side by Side

FAMILIES
LEARNING
& LIVING THE
FAITH TOGETHER

Delia Halverson

Abingdon Press
Nashville

SIDE BY SIDE
Families Learning and Living the Faith Together

Copyright © 2002 by Abingdon Press

This book is printed on recycled, acid-free, elemental-chlorine–free paper.

Library of Congress Cataloging-in-Publication Data

(CIP data has been applied for.)

ISBN 0-687-0-4911-3

To those who truly recognize the importance of families learning and living the faith:
Your time has come!

02 03 04 05 06 07 08 09 10 11 — 10 9 8 7 6 5 4 3 2 1

MANUFACTURED IN THE UNITED STATES OF AMERIC

CONTENTS

PART III: SESSION SUGGESTIONS

PART IV: HANDOUTS

INTRODUCTION

Several years ago I received a telephone call from a Christian educator, who related that a parent was bringing her son to an adult Sunday school class instead of placing him in the two-year-old class. She did not have a problem with the children's class, but instead felt guilty about the lack of time she was able to spend with her child. She worked outside the home, and Sunday was a special opportunity to be with her child. By bringing her son to class, she could at least be near him physically. At the time, I thought this situation was unique, but since then, I have learned of other such occurrences in churches across the country.

This was the dawning of a new twist on what was once called *intergenerational learning*. The purpose of such learning was simply to help the generations get to know each other. The idea is an important one, but may have arrived before its time. At the time the concept was introduced in the late 1960s and the 1970s. There was no inherent need on the part of the parents for this style of learning. Parents, particularly mothers who did not work outside the home, were in fact eager for opportunities to spend time with other adults.

Any idea that is not born of need often falls flat. This is what happened to intergenerational learning. Now however, there is an emerging need for these multiage learning experiences. Family interaction and learning has arrived and is coming of age, particularly learning opportunities for parents, grandparents, and children.

How to Use This Book

In *Side by Side* you will find information about children, youth, and parents (or other adults) and how they can benefit from learning together. In addition, you will find various formats where this learning can take place.

Side by Side also includes eighteen suggested lessons for your use, along with handouts to accompany the sessions. Since no two churches are alike, feel free to tailor the material to meet your own needs and the needs of the families in your church. Nine of these lessons are presented in lesson-plan form (that is, four Advent sessions, Ash Wednesday, Pentecost, All Saints Day, Thanksgiving, and Friendship). In addition to the sample lessons are nine session suggestions for additional topics. These additional topics had so many possible learning opportunities that I hated to choose for you. Instead, the information is presented in a way that allows you to select specific learning experiences and form them into one session or a series of sessions of any length that you choose. The session "God's Gift of Friendship" is written specifically to use with learning or activity centers, where family groups can move about freely. Take note of this as a possible format for other sessions.

Whatever you do with the material in this book, I hope your congregation will discover a growing interest in children and parents learning and sharing together. We live in a new world, and need every possible opportunity to share across the generations.

Part 1

FAMILIES

LEARNING

TOGETHER

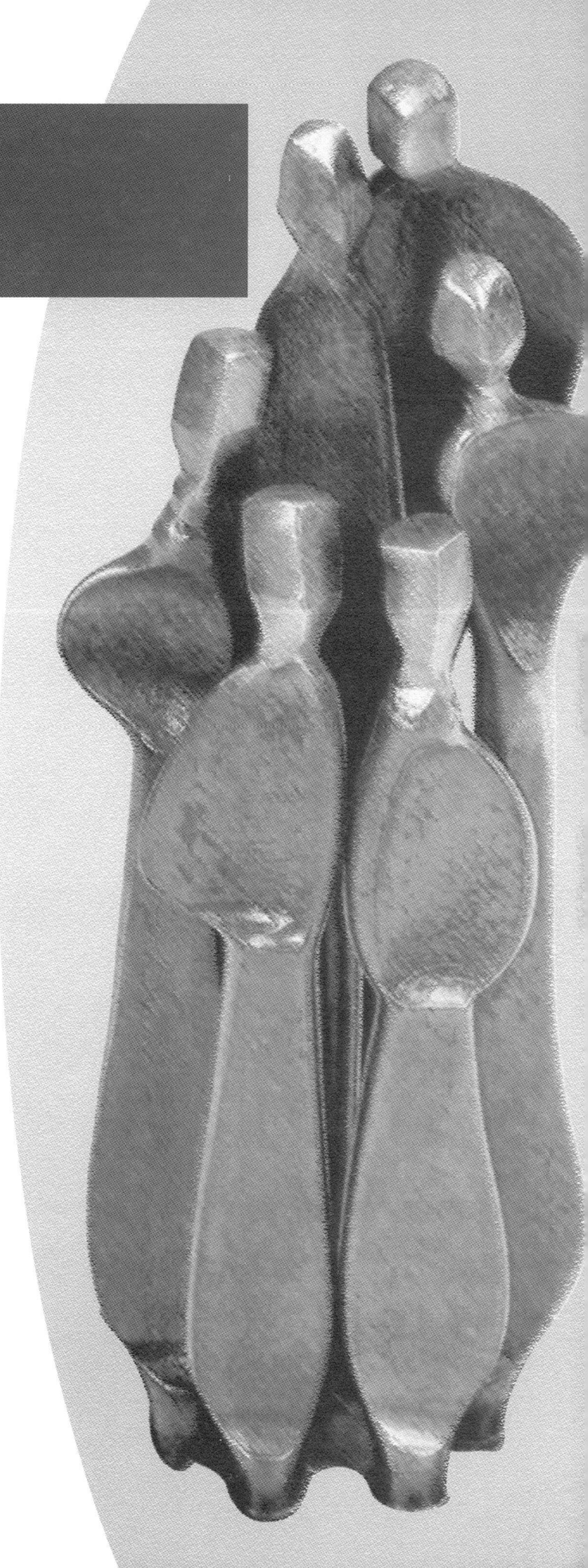

Chapter 1

Why Together?

The early church had many opportunities for learning together. In fact, the religious community of the Old Testament knew the true value of multi-age learning. From the beginning we read in Deuteronomy 6:6-9:

> Memorize his laws and tell them to your children over and over again. Talk about them all the time, whether you're at home or walking along the road or going to bed at night, or getting up in the morning. Write down copies and tie them to your wrists and foreheads to help you obey them. Write these laws on the door frames of your homes and on your gates. (CEV)

Imagine the Hebrews, as they made their way through the wilderness, sitting around the campfire in family groups in the evenings. These families were not like the typical families of today, but extended families that included children and youth of all ages, parents, grandparents, aunts, uncles, and cousins. The young child would be asleep in someone's lap, and the older child might be leaning on a shoulder. Perhaps the youth would sit together, but across the campfire they could watch a parent with eyes of understanding as the story was told. And all the while the storyteller wove the characters into the web of their own heritage. It was the legacy of the whole faith family that was on the storyteller's lips. This was "his" story and "her" story coming to life, right in the midst of all the community of faith. This was truly *their* story!

Over hundreds of years life changed, but it changed very slowly. Throughout the changes there was still opportunity after opportunity for sharing faith among generations. Living in stable communities, children found grandparents, aunts, and uncles with exciting tales to tell about the previous years. They found other adults of their parents' generation, and even their grandparents' generation, who would listen to their problems and offer suggestions. Relationships flourished and learning took place.

With the arrival of the industrial revolution, adult children began to move away from the community in which they grew up. And as science extended our life expectancy, older parents moved to retirement communities. There are no longer impromptu opportunities for mixed ages to relate to one another.

During the twentieth century we recognized the importance of age-level learning, and that was a good thing. Our educational ministry in the church has now developed around generational lines. We have learned about age level concepts and ways that various ages learn best. This has been a positive factor in our writing and selection of curriculum. However, in doing this we have let slide the opportunities for children and parents to learn together. Where else, besides the church, can generations interact so easily? But even in our churches, adults walk down the halls, looking over the heads of children, and children and youth find themselves set aside in separate wings of the building, doing kid things with only a few adults in the room.

Moreover, parents feel inadequate in sharing their faith with their children. Many of them had limited church-related learning experiences themselves, and consequently they are uncomfortable discussing faith matters. Learning and sharing the faith together in planned multi-age events can give them experiences that help them feel more comfortable with their own children in spontaneous sharing opportunities. Such events also act as learning arenas for the adults who are embarrassed to admit their lack of knowledge. When parents work in a classroom with their children, then they also learn, and the potential exists to share that learning afterward as a family.

AGE UNDERSTANDINGS

Although we will be dealing with multi-age learning in this book, it is still important to recognize various concepts and ideas that are appropriate for various ages. In such an atmosphere we do not draw sharp age lines, but we do recognize that in-depth Bible study is not appropriate for younger children. Therefore, we must deal with areas that relate to every age in some way.

For example, as adults we can grasp the abstract meaning of the story of Abraham's willingness to sacrifice Isaac. We see Abraham's actions as an expression of his understanding of God. At the time of this story other religions in the area believed in a god that required child sacrifice. Could Abraham have so strong a commitment to God that he could give up his son? These are adult, abstract concepts, but children live in a very concrete world. And so we would not use such a story with children.

Moreover, because a story is about a child does not mean it is for children. Stories for children should deal with their everyday life. For example, children will relate to the story of Zacchaeus because they know what it is like to be small and unable to see over crowds. They also know what it is like to have people make fun of them. And so when Jesus befriends Zacchaeus, they recognize and appreciate the caring attitude of Jesus.

We can use the miracle stories as a basis for family learning experiences, but we must realize that young children have nothing on which to base a miracle. For them it is a miracle that parents have food on the table when they are hungry! For children, what is more relevant in the story of Jesus feeding the multitude is that Jesus cared about the people who were hungry and saw that they had food. They can appreciate the story from that angle as a child and then later explore the miraculous aspect of it. We will, in multi-age learning, allow each age to take from the story what he or she can deal with at that level of understanding, yet not baffle them with concepts that may cause them to draw hurtful conclusions. One thing that is important for young children is to always use stories that exhibit positive behavior toward children.

Some of the same things can be said about adults in various degrees of spiritual growth. One particular story will have different meaning to different people, and that is all right. As the adults help the children in learning, their understanding also grows. There is a "learning ladder" that many educators are familiar with that says that our highest quality of learning comes when we teach others. In that manner, the parents are learning as they work side by side with their children, and are teaching in ways that they don't even realize.

> One thing that is important for young children is to always use stories that exhibit behavior toward children.

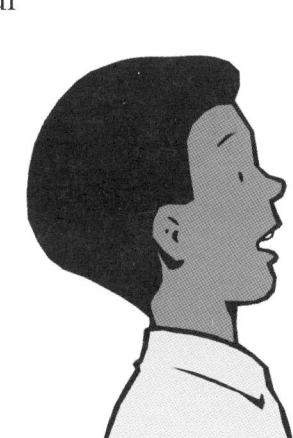
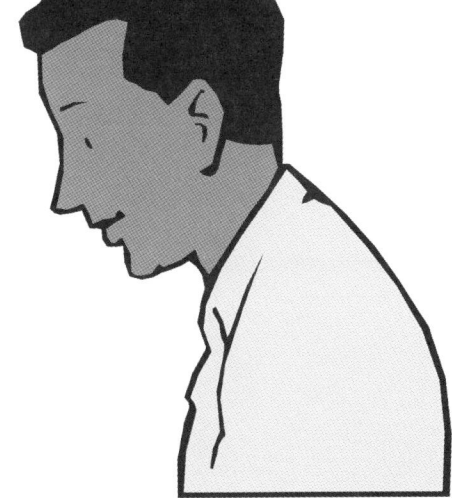

Chapter 2

Various Opportunities for Learning

The Sunday school, as we know it, began in England in the era of John Wesley, when children of the poor spent six days a week working in factories and were not able to continue (or in some cases, even begin) their formal schooling. The church leaders of that day looked at the needs of the community and began a school to teach the rudiments of learning on the only day that these children did not work, on Sundays. Often they used the Bible as the text for reading lessons, and so there was religious instruction along with the three Rs. Because this learning took place on Sunday, it became known as Sunday school.

When labor laws were passed that forbade the employment of children, and especially when free education was available, children were able to attend school during the week. The churches then turned to religious instruction on Sundays, along with the worship hour. We have followed this format of learning for over a century, until it has been drilled into our consciousness that this is the only way that religion can be taught. However, there are many formats available for the learning arena. For example, we can use our biblical heritage as a pattern, for the Hebrews taught even at the dinner table when they celebrated the Passover.

LEARNING ANY DAY OF THE WEEK

First, we must challenge the erroneous mind-set that Christian education can happen only on Sundays. Christian education happens every day of the week, whether we recognize it or not. Every time we share God's world with a child, it is a multi-age learning experience, and when we simply comment that God made the world, we have made it a religious sharing experience. Every time we tell a child "God loves with a happy heart and a sad heart, but God always loves," we have passed on a Christian concept, whether at home, in church, or while walking through the mall.

We can also look at different opportunities for planned learning experiences for parents and children. Here are a few:

- Consider a midweek supper at the church. Suggestions for this can be found in chapter 4.
- The traditional Easter egg hunt can be coupled with learning about our Easter symbols.
- Think about how acolyte training can become a multi-age experience when various members of the worship committee are involved in providing the training.
- If we include all ages in a show-me visit to a religious mission or heritage site, it becomes a unique learning experience.
- A church retreat makes a wonderful learning opportunity. Instead of separating the various ages in different locations, encourage learning through large and small group settings of mixed ages.
- When elementary children receive a Bible from the church, plan a learning experience where parents and children can explore the Bible together. Parents who have had little experience with the Bible can gather information along with their children, and with this common background they will begin to feel comfortable working and talking with the children at home.
- Inviting senior adults to act as surrogate grandparents in a preschool classroom is a good example of multi-age learning. Although the senior adults know the basics that may be the subject of the class, they will glean new learning about today's children.
- Worship is one of the best arenas for multi-age learning. Chapter 3 discusses this area in more depth.

Almost every planned event in the congregation *can* be turned into a family learning experience.

LEARNING THROUGH DOING

The most effective learning opportunities happen through actual hands-on experiences. These can include everything from making something that relates to the subject, to acting out a story; from interviewing a person about a particular subject, to actual on-site mission experiences. All of these can be done through families learning together.

If an activity such as making a friendship bracelet seems too elementary for adults, then involve them as "teachers" on a one-on-one basis. Distribute the instructions to the adults, and then ask them to work directly with one or more children.

> The most effective learning opportunities happen through actual hands-on experiences.

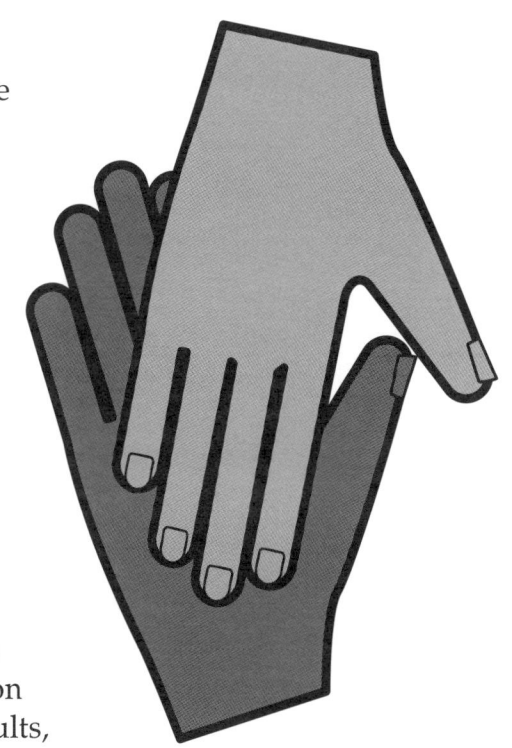

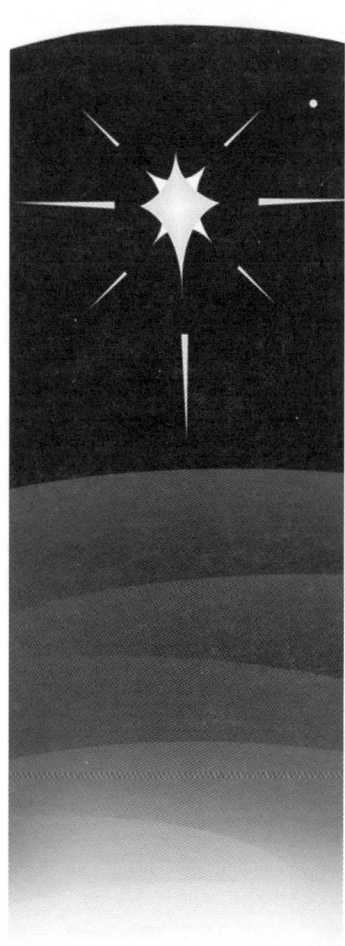

For some of the experiences, such as acting out a story, consider asking the children to participate while the adults watch. In an informal drama experience, children may act out adult parts or adults act the part of children. Or create an "observing crowd" for a scene in the story, and ask those who don't feel comfortable in "lead positions" to be a part of the crowd.

One church has a family Christmas Eve service where the story of Jesus' birth is acted out by all who want to participate. Everyone is invited to come dressed as a character they would like to portray. Additional simple costumes (headpieces, shepherd's staffs, crowns, and so on) are available for those who do not have one but want to be a part of the drama. Then when a particular character enters the story, all those who choose to be that character come forward. They may have twenty Marys and five shepherds, but everyone becomes the character he or she wants to portray, and the story is lived out among the congregation.

The main object in these situations is to recognize that *the learning comes through the doing*. We are not looking for a finished product in the performing arts, but instead the opportunity to make the story or the situation a part of the learner's life.

Teenagers may sometimes feel that an activity is too childish for them. If so, then involve them as "teachers," stage hands, or in passing out the equipment. Youth also enjoy being official photographers of a session. As long as they are in the group and feel included, they will grasp some learning of what's happening. The main learning component is involvement, which is how the learning takes place.

Finally, special hands-on projects and mission experiences are excellent ways for children and parents to learn together. See chapter 6 for more specific information.

Chapter 3

Learning Through Worship

Unfortunately, worship and education have been divorced for too long. Moreover, we have come to see the congregation in corporate worship as an audience. In true worship, God is the audience, we, the worshipers, are the actors, and the pastors and musicians act as prompters as well as actors. When we look at worship in this manner, then all ages can take an active part. We remove the performance attitude and foster involvement.

Our attitude of acceptance of children in the worship service makes a difference in whether learning takes place. Some churches have created miniature worship services for children, separate and apart from the adults. They believe that they are "training" the children for participation in the "big" worship service. In reality, this separate service simply tells the children that they are not accepted among the adults and must learn the correct lines before they can be a part of the drama. There is a window of time in the life of children when it is exciting for them to be a part of what their parents do. That window usually closes at about the fourth grade. If we push them aside during the years just prior to that, it is hard to involve them later.

Sometimes children learn from adults, and many times adults learn from children. I have learned many a lesson from children in the "Children's Time" during the worship service. These few minutes can be effective opportunities for adults and children to learn side by side. To enable this learning we must not talk over the children's heads or ask cutesy questions of them that brings out answers that will elicit laughter from the adults. We also don't want children's time to become a show-off time. Children need to be recognized as legitimate worshipers, who are seeking answers and an opportunity to worship God just as adults.

Dick Murray, a past professor of Christian education at Perkins School of Theology in Dallas, told the story of his experience with his

grandson. As the story goes, when he and his three-year-old grandson were driving the streets of Dallas they would sing Gloria Patri. He would sit in the front seat singing, "Glory be to the Father" and his grandson would sit in his car seat in the back singing, "Glory Paw-Paw. Glory, Paw-Paw." One Sunday they were worshiping together, and when the congregation stood up to sing the Gloria Patri, his grandson pulled on his jacket and said, "Paw-Paw, they're singing our song!"

Dick's point was that children need to learn some of the basics of worship even though they don't understand it. They need to feel that acceptance in the family of God. They need to know that we are singing "their song." They will grasp what they can understand in the beginning, adding to it as the years pass. It is important for them to have opportunities to be with worshipers of all ages.

I enjoyed a family worship service one Sunday in Austin, Texas. The regular traditional service was happening at the same time in the sanctuary. As they did each Sunday, we gathered in the chapel which had been remodeled to make it more versatile, using chairs instead of pews and making the worship table and lecterns movable. For this service, the chairs were placed in curved rows, facing the worship table and lectern that were in front of the lovely stained glass windows on the side of the chapel. The multi-age choir sat in the area that was normally the chancel. When it was time for the scripture to be read, a father and his three-year-old son walked up to the front. The young boy could not read, but he held his father's hand as the man read. Children assisted their parents in passing out bulletins and taking the offering, and the pastor made sure that her sermon was filled with illustrations that related to all ages. We forget that the one common ground that we all have is that of being a child. Any story that

> We forget that the one common ground that we all have is that of having had a childhood.

involves childhood experiences is one that we all feel comfortable with, no matter what the age. In this particular service, only a few of the children had leadership parts, but every child there felt a part of the leadership. Children can live a part vicariously as they sit in the pew. If another child is involved, then they feel involvement too.

One of the best learning opportunities for parents and children is right in the pew during a worship service. Parents are seldom aware of this, and instead of using this as a learning opportunity they struggle with keeping the child quiet and in place. They are also at quite a loss about how to initiate that learning, that opportunity to truly worship together as parent and child.

As leaders in Christian education we can help in a couple of ways. First, we can plan a study about worship that facilitates parents and children learning together. On page 118 you will find a model of such a study. But beyond that, a young reader's bulletin is a very effective teaching tool. This is different from the children's bulletin that many publishers produce. The published children's bulletins are learning tools that, although they approach the subject and text of the day, are seldom interactive with the service itself. A young reader's bulletin, on the other hand, focuses the child's attention on the acts of worship as they occur. It follows the particular form of worship for your congregation and intersperses definitions of what is going on. It has built-in opportunities for reflections and notes, so that the reader becomes involved in the action between God and the people. To develop a young reader's bulletin, use the format on page 18 and adapt it to your own congregational worship.

One of the best learning opportunities for parents and children is right in the pew during a worship service.

Young Reader's Bulletin ·····························

_____ Church

Hometown, USA

_____
date

Before the service begins:
1. Greet people around you before the prelude begins.
2. As the music begins, listen quietly and prepare for worship.
3. Locate the hymns in your hymnal and mark them.
4. Locate the scripture in the pew Bible and mark the place.
5. Fill in the name of someone or something you want to pray about during Morning Prayers.
6. Look for the asterisk (*) to know when we stand.
7. Give a smile of love to your parent(s).
8. Pray for those who lead us and that God helps us worship.

PRELUDE *(We prepare for worship. Listen to the music and think of God's love.)*

CONCERNS OF THE CHURCH
(Write or draw something mentioned to remember this week. Be sure to remind your parents that Wednesday pick-up time is now 7:50 P.M. sharp.)

MEDITATION AND SILENT CONFESSION
(Think of something you have done wrong that you want to change. Write or draw it here.) ✎

RESPONSE TO GOD'S GIVING

*Doxology
Praise God from whom all blessings flow.
Praise him all creatures here below.
Praise him above ye heavenly hosts.
Praise Father, Son, and Holy Ghost. Amen.

Offertory *(We give God some of what God has given us. As the organ plays, write or draw a special good thing that happened to you this week.)* . . . . ✎

 **SCRIPTURE** Matthew 28:16-20 Page 967
(Listen to and read the scripture. This is a special command that Jesus gave everyone who is to follow him. What does Jesus say we are to do? How does Jesus say he will help us to do this?)

MINISTRY OF MUSIC Chancel Choir
(Listen to the words of the anthem and draw a picture that explains what the words say.) . . . . ✎

CALL TO WORSHIP (from John 1)
Leader: In the beginning was the Word, and the Word was with God, and the Word was God.
People: In him was life and the life was the light of all.
Leader: The light shines in the darkness and the darkness has not overcome it.
People: The true light that enlightens everyone was coming into the world.

18

*HYMN 53 . . . . *Fairest Lord Jesus*

*PRAYER OF INVOCATION AND OUR LORD'S PRAYER
Our Father, who art in heaven, hallowed be thy name. Thy kingdom come, thy will be done on earth as it is in heaven. Give us this day our daily bread. And forgive us our trespasses, as we forgive those who trespass against us. And lead us not into temptation, but deliver us from evil. For thine is the kingdom, and the power, and the glory, forever. Amen.

*GLORIA PATRI
Glory be to the Father, and to the Son, and to the Holy Ghost.
As it was in the beginning, is now, and ever shall be.
World without end. Amen. Amen.

CHILDREN'S CHOIR
(Your time to lead the people in praising God.)

CHILDREN'S MOMENT *(Join the pastor in the front.)*

MORNING PRAYERS

PRELUDE TO PRAYER   #438 . . . . *Seek Ye First*
Moment of Silent Prayer
(Remember persons for whom you specially want to pray. Write the names below.)

_____   _____   _____

_____   _____   _____

THE MESSAGE   *(The Pastor)*
To Grow in Christ and to Make Christ Known
*(Listen as the pastor explains what we pledge
to do as a part of our church. Write or draw
something you can do to "grow in Christ" or
to become a better Christian.)* . . . . ✏

*HYMN 497 . . . . *O Zion Haste*

*BENEDICTION
(The pastor sends us into the world to live as God wants us to live.)

*CONGREGATIONAL RESPONSE
In Christ there is no east or west,
in him no south or north;
but one great fellowship of love
throughout the whole wide earth.

CHOIR RECESSIONAL

POSTLUDE
*(As you leave, remember that God is with you through
the week. Don't forget Sunday school at 10:15 A.M.)*

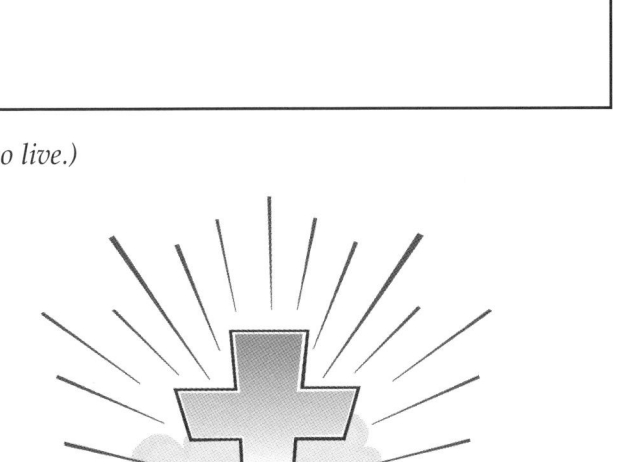

As a congregation, we can learn about worship in various other ways. Something as simple as regularly placing a statement about worship in your bulletin can be an effective learning tool. Look at your worship service and around your sanctuary, then write two or three brief statements about worship or the symbols and colors in the sanctuary. These can be explanations of symbols and colors, or they can be simple questions, such as "Did you know that we stand for the first hymn in the same manner that people stand when a king enters the room? We look at Christ as our King." Placing these statements and questions in the bulletin each week, offers a learning tool for all ages.

Sometimes we become so stuck in a worship routine that we forget that different people come to spirituality in different ways, no matter what their age. The early church used several senses in worship including sight, sound, smell, taste, and feeling. Visuals are great learning tools for worship. The stained glass windows were first used to recall the Bible stories for the people who could not read. In addition, symbols, banners, and worship centers are also great tools for visual learning. Early church leaders used the other senses to teach those gathered about worship and its importance. For example, incense was used in the early church to enhance the learning process, and some churches use it even today. The communion elements made and still make use of our sense of taste, while the early church (as well as some traditions today) implemented learning special prayers by use of rosary beads. Singing, bells and other sound instruments have been a part of the audio learning in the church for many years.

Another early church learning tool was drama. Every age can enjoy and participate in drama. When drama is used, even those persons who are not physically participating become a part of the experience. Unfortunately, drama lost much of its appeal when the church moved to North America and took on a more solemn nature. In some churches it has been relegated to the fellowship hall and ministries with children and youth. Because of this it has

"Did you know that we stand for the first hymn in the same manner that people stand when a king enters the room? We look at Christ as our King."

become more of a performance than a tool to enhance worship. However, it is definitely a learning tool we should consider as a part of worship. Drama can reenact a story from the Bible, or depict a concept or theme for worship. It might be spoken or sung, or it might simply use actions. It can be used as a way to engage both the audio and visual senses.

Special services and celebrations also provide opportunities to learn in multi-age communities of faith. The major celebration for the early church was Easter. On that day each year the early church not only celebrated the Resurrection, but also confirmed new members of the faith.

We can and do continue this early church tradition of learning in several ways. During the four Sundays of Advent we often include intergenerational activities and learning time, when various ages participate in the lighting of an Advent wreath. This can be as simple as reading scripture or as informative as explaining a part of our waiting period of Advent. Some churches even include congregational participation through a litany during this service. Other special seasonal celebrations might include Epiphany, Pentecost, All Saints Day, and Ascension Sunday.

One of my favorite ways to use special Sundays is to build the whole worship service around the learning. For example, a "Hanging of the Greens" service can become a way to introduce the meaning of our traditional decorations, explaining them as they are placed in the sanctuary.

> Special services and celebrations also provide opportunities to learn in multi-age communities of faith.

Hanging of the Greens

This service takes very little time during the corporate worship because the learning is woven into the regular order of worship. People of all ages have opportunity to participate. Use this as a design and adjust it according to your usual litany of worship.

After the Prelude
Leader: *The prophet Isaiah wrote, "Prepare the way of the Lord." Let us prepare our worship area as we prepare our hearts for the coming of Christ.* (Dim the lights.)

After Introit (with lights dimmed)
Leader: *The world sat in darkness, waiting for the light.*
ALL: OUR LORD, WE AWAIT YOUR COMING. WE RECOGNIZE OUR NEED FOR YOUR FORGIVENESS AND YOUR LOVE.
(Brief silence for personal reflection.)
Choir: "Morning Has Broken"—as the choir sings, the tree lights are lighted.

Processional Hymn "Joyful, Joyful, We Adore Thee" (Lights are raised. Congregation stands.)

Call to Worship (During this reading garlands are brought up the aisles and hung as planned.)
Leader: *God placed vegetation on the earth to sustain us and to renew the earth. Our plants give us food and shelter, and through their humus the soil is renewed.*
ALL: THANK YOU, GOD, FOR YOUR PLAN FOR RENEWED LIFE. THANK YOU FOR CHRIST WHO GIVES US NEW LIFE.
Leader: *As the green plants take in carbon dioxide and give off oxygen, the air on which we depend is renewed.*
ALL: WE COME TO THIS ADVENT SEASON ANTICIPATING THE RENEWAL OF YOUR COVENANT THROUGH CHRIST.
Leader: *As the evergreen tree is forever green, so we know that we can depend on God's love forever. We also know that through Christ's life we can experience life eternal.*
ALL: AS YOU GIVE US ETERNAL LIFE, WE PLEDGE OUR CONSTANT LOVE AND SERVICE TO YOU.

Placement of Wreaths (After reading, special music or hymn may be sung as wreaths are completed.)

Leader: *The circle has no beginning and no end. God's love also has no beginning and no end. The red bows represent the ultimate sacrifice, when Jesus gave his life for us.*

Lighting Advent Candle

Children's Moment (Children invited to come to front for Advent Affirmation of Faith and explanations of the Chrismons. The Chrismons are placed on tree during the reading and anthem.)

Advent Affirmation of Faith

ALL: WE BELIEVE IN THE ONE TRUE GOD, ALMIGHTY AND GREATER THAN ANY KING CLOTHED IN PURPLE AND GOLD.

Leader: *In the ancient world, purple was a scarce color and therefore used by royalty. The color of Advent is purple, reminding us of the royalty of Christ. The crown reminds us that Jesus Christ is king of our lives.*

ALL: WE BELIEVE THAT GOD CAME TO US IN HUMAN FORM, AS MESSIAH AND SAVIOR OF ALL THE WORLD.

Leader: *The shepherd's crook reminds us of those shepherds who first visited the Christ Child, and that Jesus told stories of how God cares for us as a shepherd. The star reminds us of the night when angels sang and a brilliant star marked the birth of Jesus, our promised Messiah.*

ALL: WE BELIEVE IN GOD, REVEALED IN THREE WAYS BUT TRULY ONE.

Leader: *The Greek letters on our tree represent various names for Jesus: Christ, Savior, Son of God. The first and last letters of the Greek alphabet, alpha and omega, remind us that Christ is with us from the beginning to the end.*

ALL: WE BELIEVE THAT CHRIST DIED FOR US, SO THAT WE MIGHT LIVE FOREVER.

Leader: *The various crosses remind us of that death.*

ALL: WE BELIEVE THAT CHRIST SENT A COMFORTER TO BE WITH US, EVEN AFTER HIS DEATH.

Leader: *Jesus told us to be fishers of people. The fish represents Christians who kept their faith during the times of persecution. They used the fish as a secret symbol so that we might know about Christ today.*

ALL: WE BELIEVE THAT CHRIST CALLS US TO FOLLOW HIM TODAY.

Gloria Patri

Anthem

Scripture Reading and Prayers

Placing of Crèche

Leader: *The villagers of Greccio, Italy, in 1223, stood in awe as a dark, dismal cave came to life with the Christmas story. Saint Francis of Assisi envisioned this method of telling the story of Christ's birth with a live manger scene, complete with animals. Today we use the crèche to remind us that the story is real.*

ALL: THANK YOU, GOD, FOR COMING IN HUMAN FORM. THROUGH CHRIST WE UNDERSTAND YOU BETTER.

Leader: *Although the shepherds and wise men came at different times, we include them both in our manger scene. This reminds us that Christ came for all of us, no matter what our circumstances.*

Hymn   "Away in a Manger"

Receiving of Tithes and Offerings

Leader: *As Christ comes to each of us, we must share Christ with others. Through our gifts and talents we share Christ.*

(For the remainder of the service follow the usual form. Any additional decorations may be added during the next week.)

Delia Halverson, *Nuts and Bolts of Christian Education* (Nashville: Abingdon Press, 1999), pp. 89-90. Used by permission.

Chapter 4

Church Supper Learning Suggestions

Midweek suppers have become a popular regular event in many churches. They serve as a format for a variety of learning experiences, including Bible study opportunities, choir rehearsals, and various classes. We must, however, take care that we do not simply bring families together for the meal only to divide them again for study. Consider planning short-term multi-age learning opportunities around the tables or as a group during the meals. This time can also include celebrations of birthdays and anniversaries, announcements (presented in interesting ways), group singing, a blessing for the food, and prayer requests.

Drama
At some point during or at the close of the meal, include a brief drama. This may be a drama about a Bible story or expressing a specific theme. The drama does not need to be elaborate and can be done in a "play reading" format where the cast members read their parts as they act them out in front of the learners. Another effective method for such an informal setting is to place several stools or chairs where the "actors" sit for the readings.

Monologues
A monologue is a one-person presentation, usually depicting a biblical character. There are prepared monologues, but more often it is effective for the presenter to make a study of the character and situation and then prepare the monologue tailored to that particular situation. The character may or may not be an actual Bible character. It can also be someone who "might-have-been" on-site, perhaps a bystander, or someone who learned about the event from someone else.

Puppet Show
Puppets offer great opportunities for parents and children to learn side by side. Some churches have puppet troupes made up primarily of adults and teens who handle elaborate puppets. The simple puppets can be just as effective, and when they are used spontaneously by people who volunteer on the spot then the other members feel more

> Consider planning short-term multi-age learning opportunities around the tables or as a group during the meals.

involved and have the attitude "That might have been me up there!" Spontaneous puppeteers can be used for familiar Bible stories, or they can be asked to respond to various subjects or questions. Behind the guise of a puppet, people often feel more comfortable expressing themselves and discussing their faith. (For example, see the puppet method used on page 74 in the Thanksgiving session.)

Scripture Sculpture

The scripture sculpture lends itself to multi-age participation. For this, ask a small group of people to depict a scene from a Bible story by using their bodies (with no words) in sculpture positions. If there are fewer main characters than group members, have the additional persons act as bystanders. As a group they will decide just who will be which character and how they might stand or sit to depict that particular scene. Then they will position themselves for that scene. They may also use simple props that are readily accessible. They might stay in position for the reading of the scripture, or you might choose to use various scenes and pause in reading the scripture as the next group moves into position.

Another way of using scripture sculpture is to ask each group to quietly select a Bible story to depict and then get in position. Have those gathered for dinner guess the story.

Small Group Research

Research is a very effective teaching method. At specific tables, place several research books and a card with a particular subject. The people at the table can look up the subject and learn about it. Then they can share their findings with the whole group at some point during the evening. Their assignment might be to discover more about an aspect of Hebrew life during Bible days, or uncover background on the people or the geography of a mission project that your congregation supports. Or it could be the history of a hymn or Christmas carol, or an aspect of church history.

> Behind the guise of a puppet, people often feel more comfortable expressing themselves and discussing their faith.

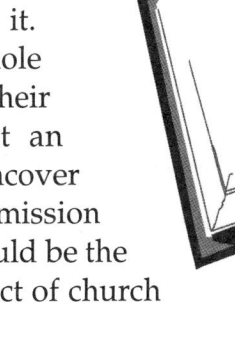

Table Discussions

Table discussions not only provide learning opportunities but also help those eating together to become better acquainted. To stimulate the discussion, provide a question or two to help break the ice. Here are some suggestions:

▶ What is your favorite Bible story and when did you first hear it?
▶ If you were able to be one character out of the Bible (or out of a specific story you are studying), which would you choose and why?
▶ What is your favorite part of a worship service? What do you like about it?
▶ Tell about something that happened this week that made you realize that God works through people.
▶ Tell about some time when someone has forgiven you for something you did wrong.

Create a Collage

Distribute magazines, poster board, scissors, and glue to each table. Using a theme that your church is considering or a seasonal theme, ask each table to create a collage of pictures for display in the church building. You might title the collage ahead of time or ask the table to decide on a title. This is a good activity for discussion of the gifts and talents that God has given each of us, perhaps around a stewardship theme. It also is a good learning activity for expressing our thankfulness at Thanksgiving.

Ask each table to create a collage of pictures for display in the church building.

Chapter 5

Adapting Curriculum

There are many formats that may be followed in multi-age learning. Some denominational publishers produce curriculum for small churches that can easily be used with children and parents. One example is the "One Room Sunday School" curriculum, which is published by Cokesbury. I know of a church that even adapted the "God and Me" curriculum from the God and Country Award program with Boy Scouts and used it for a Sunday school class during the summer months for families with elementary aged children. *Faith Home: Families Growing Together in Faith*, a study from Abingdon Press, is designed for several two hour sessions. However, it can be adapted to more sessions with shorter time frames. Bridge Resources has published *Grand Friends Young Friends*, a mentoring program for older adults and older children with a leader guide and participants' book. In addition, Group Publishers offers *Family Sunday School Fun—13 Bible Lessons for Children & Parents*. These resources along with the sessions provided here will get you started.

However, you do not have to rely on curriculum written specifically for family or multi-age learning. Instead consider adapting the third and fourth grade curriculum that your congregation presently uses. Almost any activity that is suggested for this age range can be done in a mixed age setting, with the adults in the group assisting the children. The following adaptation of parts of the summer 2001 edition of the *Exploring Faith* curriculum will give you additional suggestions of how curriculum can be adapted.

PRINTED PLAN	ADAPTED PLAN
FOOD IN BIBLE TIMES	**FOOD IN BIBLE TIMES**
Bountiful Bread	**Bountiful Bread**
Greet the children as they arrive. Play the music (Cassette/CD) from the lesson as the children come into the room. Give each child the attendance sticker for today and show the students where to place it on the attendance chart.	Greet the learners as they arrive. Play the music (Cassette/CD) from the lesson as the learners come into the room. Give each person the attendance sticker for today and show them where to place it on the attendance chart.

ASK: What is your favorite kind of bread? What is your least favorite kind of bread? Did you know that bread is eaten by people all over the world?

Set out a variety of breads for the children to taste. Include breads such as matzo crackers, pita bread, whole wheat bread, tortillas, rice cakes, french bread, rye bread, rolls, muffins, biscuits, scones, and so forth. Cut the breads into small bite size pieces and let the children have a "tasting." Let the children indicate what their favorite kinds of bread might be.

Plowing, Sowing, Planting
Say: Bible-times people had to grow most of the food they ate. There were no refrigerators or ways of preserving food from day to day. So everything had to be eaten when it was ripe or it spoiled. Bread after one day was usually stale. Fish after one day spoiled. Grapes were dried to make raisins. Figs were also dried to preserve them.

Say: Farmers used oxen to plow their fields. But not every farmer had an ox with a plow, so families shared. Plowing was very hard work. Fields were much smaller in Bible times because they did not have the farming equipment that we have today.

To Market, to Market
(Here the curriculum suggests the children make a marketplace using clay, fabric, etc.)

Golan Discs
(Here the curriculum suggests that they make a simple bread that can be baked in a toaster oven.)

Bread from Heaven!
(The curriculum suggests that low tables be set and the bread eaten along with other biblical foods, such as raisins, figs, cheese, and olives, giving a thank-you prayer before eating.)

Divide into groups: Divide the class into "family groups," keeping family units together, but being sure persons without other members of their family are incorporated into a group. Ask the family groups to discuss their favorite and least favorite kinds of bread. Remind them that bread is eaten by people all over the world.

Give the family groups an opportunity to taste a variety of breads, including matzo crackers, pita bread, whole wheat bread, tortillas, rice cakes, french bread, rye bread, rolls, muffins, biscuits, scones, or such, and discuss which they like best.

Plowing, Sowing, Planting
Ask the family groups to discuss the answers to the following questions about Bible-times:
Ask:
- In Bible-times there were no trucks and trains to transport food. Where do you suppose they got their food?
- There were no refrigerators or other ways to preserve food. What difference do you suppose this made in their eating habits?

In family groups ask the learners to discuss the following questions.
- There was no big equipment to plow the fields of the farmers. How did they plow fields to plant? Did this make a difference in the size of their fields?

To Market, to Market
(A marketplace like that suggested in the curriculum can be easily made by family groups.)

Golan Discs
(A simple bread can be made in family groups.)

Bread from Heaven!
(The bread can be eaten at low tables along with other biblical foods, such as raisins, figs, cheese, and olives. Learners may sit either in family groups or as a large group, giving a

(The curriculum offers discussion of how God fed the people of Israel with manna and quail when they were hungry, and then the story is listened to on a cassette/CD.)

"I Am the Bread"

Bring the children together in the worship or storytelling area. Teach them the American Sign Language for the verse:

I—The "I" hand (little finger extended, all others folded down) is placed at the chest.

am—/fingers and thumb are folded down into a loose fist, placed in front of the face, and moved forward slightly.

the bread—Place the left hand in front of the body, fingers pointing right; draw the little finger side of the right hand down the back of the left hand several times.

of—Hook the right index finger and thumb into the left index finger and thumb.

life—Place the "FIVE" hands near the waist and draw the hands up, wiggling the fingers.

Say: In today's lesson we have talked about the kinds of food eaten by Bible-times people. We have learned that of all the different foods, bread was probably the most important part of their everyday diet. Bread was so special in fact that it was never even cut with a knife. It was always broken. When Jesus told his disciples, "I am the bread of life" they knew exactly what he meant, because bread was so important.

Once the children have mastered the signs, let them "pass the signs" around the circle. The

thank-you prayer before eating.)

(In a multi-age setting you can still have discussion of how God fed the people of Israel with manna and quail when they were hungry, and then listen to the story on a cassette/CD.)

"I Am the Bread"
(The multi-age class can easily learn the signing to the verse, and then all pass the sign around the circle. If it is a large group, this can be done in family groups.)

first child in the circle will make the sign for "I" and turn to the child on his or her right. That child will make the sign for "I am" and turn to the child on his or her right. Continue around the circle until the verse is completed and then start again. (Note: Articles such as "a," "an," or "the" are rarely signed and have been combined with their nouns.)

Pass the Bread, Please

Ask: What do you think Jesus meant when he said, "I am the bread of life?" (Invite the children to share their ideas.)

Stuff a small brown paper lunch bag with recycled newspaper to resemble a loaf of brown bread. Have the children sit in a circle.

Say: Jesus is the bread of life. Jesus taught his friends that if they would just follow God's laws, then God would provide them all that they needed. As we play the music, we will gently toss this "loaf of bread" around the circle to each other. Then when music stops, whoever is holding the "bread" will say "thank you" for some gift that God has given.

Play the game as long as time allows or until the children are having difficulty thinking of things God has given them. Then sing "God's Children" together.

Pray: Thank you God for Jesus, who is the bread of life. Help us to listen to his teachings and know that he wants us to be closer to you. Amen.

Pass the Bread, Please

(This closing activity can easily be done in a multi-age grouping.)

Jesus is the bread of life. Jesus taught his friends that if they would just follow God's laws, then God would provide them all that they needed.

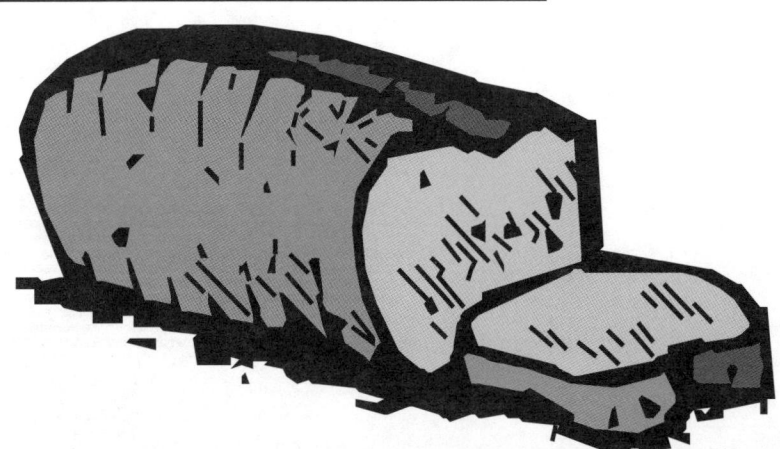

Chapter 6

Projects and Mission Opportunities

In Mark 12:29-31, Jesus reminded the Sadducees of the commandment to love neighbor as self. In John 15:12-17, Jesus asks us to bear the fruit of love for one another. And at the close of Matthew (28:19-20) Jesus gave us the Great Commission, to make disciples of all nations. What better opportunity to carry out these commands of Jesus but in our families! Below are some possibilities to do just that.

Grow a garden—There are several options here. You may want to raise food that can be shared with a food kitchen or families who are in need. Growing a multicultural garden not only gives an experience of mission, but also introduces us to food of other cultures.

Supply a meal—This may be done through a local mission or by locating a family in need of food and inviting them to share a meal. You can also be in mission by taking a meal to persons who are coming home from the hospital and unable to fix a meal for themselves.

Another idea is to make bag or box lunches for people working on projects such as a Habitat for Humanity house.

Bake for others—Many homeless shelters would enjoy home baked bread and/or cookies. This is an activity where all ages can participate (such as stirring, kneading, decorating, and so forth).

Share song/friendship/pet—Arrange with local nursing homes or retirement facilities for an intergenerational visit. Younger families might also arrange to deliver a cassette tape of the church service to a specific shut-in each week and spend time getting to know the person. Often homebound adults or children enjoy having your pets visit with you, but be sure to check for approval. St. Marks United Methodist Church in Lincoln, Nebraska, has a program called PAWS (Pets Are Working Saints) where pets visit in local nursing homes.

> In John 15:12-17, Jesus asks us to bear the fruit of love for one another.

Visit mission sites—Find out locations of church mission sites near your community or elsewhere and arrange for families to visit. These might even include overnight trips.

Adopt a room/garden space—Ask family groups to adopt a church classroom or a specific area around the church. Have them apply their decorating talents to their room, or gardening know-how to a plot of earth.

Plant a tree—Arrange to plant a tree in a park or along a roadway to refurbish the earth. Or raise money for trees to be replanted in the rainforests that have been destroyed.

Pray for missionaries and their children—Send for calendars that list the birthdays of missionary children and adults. Pray for those who are listed each day, and write to them on their birthday. (For information about the calendars, contact the General Board of Global Ministries Service Center, 7820 Reading Road, Caller No. 1800, Cincinnati, OH 45222-1800.)

Plan a Souper Bowl—Arrange to collect money for a local soup kitchen on Super Bowl Sunday, using a soup kettle to collect. Call Spring Valley Presbyterian Church, 125 Sparkleberry Lane, Columbia, SC 29223 (800-358-SOUP) for more information.

Intergenerational work camp—Several churches have sponsored multigenerational work camps that do construction work, and provide Vacation Bible School leadership. In addition, consider the organizations listed below for some possibilities. The following churches also have experience with intergenerational camps:

St. Paul's United Methodist Church
5501 Main, Houston, TX 77004
(713) 528-0527

First United Methodist Church
116 NE Perry Ave., Peoria, IL 61603-3687
(309) 673-3641

ORGANIZATIONS

Appalachia Service Project, 4523 Bristol Hwy., Piney Flats, TN 37686-5201 This is a repair/home building ministry for economically disadvantaged people, using a Christian perspective. Provides materials for

> Arrange to plant a tree in a park or along a roadway to refurbish the earth.

study ahead of time, and intergenerational opportunities are available. One week during the summer and a weekend in the spring are set aside specifically for families (ages 6 years and up). Other weekends may be arranged.

Bethesda Learning Center Work Camp, P.O. Box 538, Bethesda, OH 43719-0538, (614) 484-4705.

Provides work camps for youth and adults, and considering the possibility of camps for families.

Children's Fund for Christian Mission, P.O. Box 840, Nashville, TN 37202.

Provides information about specific missions and encourages all ages to contribute to this fund.

CROP (an ecumenical organization which provides food, seeds, tools, and various other kinds of appropriate technology to those without)—Church World Service, P.O. Box 968, Elkhart, Indiana 46515.

They provide hunger educational materials and design a CROP Walk every year to raise money for hunger. All ages often participate in the Walk. (A project of United Methodist Committee on Relief.)

ECHO (Educational Concerns for Hunger Organization), 17430 Durrance Rd., North Ft. Myers, FL 33917-2200 www.echonet.org 1-772-543-3246.

Uses volunteer help to research, develop, and distribute seeds and information on trees, edible plants, and small animals to countries in need. Also provides intern training and networking newsletter for missionaries and other nonprofit workers in Third World countries. (A project of United Methodist Committee on Relief.) Also has Vacation Bible School program and has materials on edible landscaping. You may secure seeds for experimenting in your own garden.

Free The Children International, P.O. Box 32099, Hartford, Connecticut 06150-2099. www.freethechildren.org

This organization was founded by a twelve-year-old (Craig Kielburger) who learned of slavery in Pakistan. There are also headquarters in Canada, Germany, Brazil, Japan, and India. Local groups can be established. Only children under the age of 18 can vote on decisions, but older youth and adults act as mentors. Over 100,000 active youth in 27 countries have helped construct over 100 schools and two live-in rehabilitation centers for children. They have built a health center in Nicaragua and distributed over a million dollars of medical supplies and 40,000 school kits.

Friends of the Americas, an organization through which you may send a Christmas box to children and families who live in economically

> ECHO uses volunteer help to research, develop, and distribute seeds and information on trees, edible plants, and small animals to countries in need.

depressed areas of Latin America. For information on the Christmas Box Project, contact Friends of the Americas, 1024 North Foster Drive, Baton Rouge, LA 70806.

Gleaning Network (includes Potato Project), Society of St. Andrew, State Rt. 615, P.O. Box 329, Big Island, VA 24526 1-800-333-4597.
Program to glean fresh produce from fields that would otherwise be plowed under. (Some projects include multi-age groups.)

Habitat for Humanity International (also Global Village Work Camp), 121 Habitat Street, Americus, GA 31709 (800) 422-4828
Older teens can participate, and some projects include families with elementary children.

Heifer Project International, P.O. Box 808, Little Rock, AR 72203
Assists poor families in rural areas throughout the world to produce more food and income for themselves with improved livestock. A curriculum (notebook of stories, activities, and information) is now available from Heifer Project International. This is a fun project for all ages to learn about and sponsor. You can give specific amounts to purchase specific animals.

Heifer Project, assists poor families in rural areas throughout the world to produce more food and income for themselves with improved livestock.

Mountain TOP (Tennessee Outreach Project), 2704 Twelfth Ave. S., Nashville, TN 37204 (615) 298-1575.
A ministry to people in need in Tennessee. They have fall weekend events where youth and adults work together.

National Arbor Day Foundation, 100 Arbor Ave., Nebraska City, NE 68410 (402) 474-5655. Planting trees to improve our world.

Potato Project, P.O. Box 329, State Rt. 615, Big Island, VA 24526 (804) 299-5956. This project salvages vegetables left in the fields after commercial pickers have finished. Because the picking is done through volunteer labor, the food can be delivered to the hungry for 1 cent per serving. You may purchase coloring books to advertise the project. All ages participate in this project.

Red Bird Mission, Queendale Center, Beverly, KY 40913. Phone: 606/598-5915 Website: http://www.gbgm-umc.org/redbirdconference. This is a missionary conference of The United Methodist Church. You may get information about projects to support this mission and opportunities for work camps.

Save Our Streams (SOS). A part of the Izaak Walton League of America, 1401 Wilson Blvd., Level B, Arlington, VA 22209 (703-528-1818).

From them you may learn how to conserve, maintain, protect, and restore the soil, forest, water, and other resources.

Shoeboxes for Liberty. Friends of the Americas, 912 N. Forest Drive, Baton Rouge, LA 70806.

Send for guidelines for boxes to pack for those in need.

Trevor's Campaign (blankets for homeless), Trevor's Place, 1624 West Popular Street, Philadelphia, PA 19130 (215) 236-4660.

This campaign began when a young boy saw homeless people on TV and wanted to help.

Trinity Braille Ministry, Trinity United Methodist Church, 3104 W. Glendale Ave., Phoenix, AZ 85051.

All-volunteer group which prepares braille copies of selected United Methodist church school literature.

UMCOR (United Methodist Committee on Relief), 475 Riverside Dr., New York, NY 10115. Hotline for current needs and opportunities 1-800-841-1235.

Projects involving refugees, agriculture, disasters, forest reclamation, hunger, and more. Help by raising money for a particular project or through Volunteers in Mission (VIM). Families with teens have participated in work teams, even overseas. Volunteer hot line 800-918-3100.

UMCOR helps with projects involving refugees, agriculture, disasters, forest reclamation, hunger, and more.

Part 2

PLANNED
SESSIONS

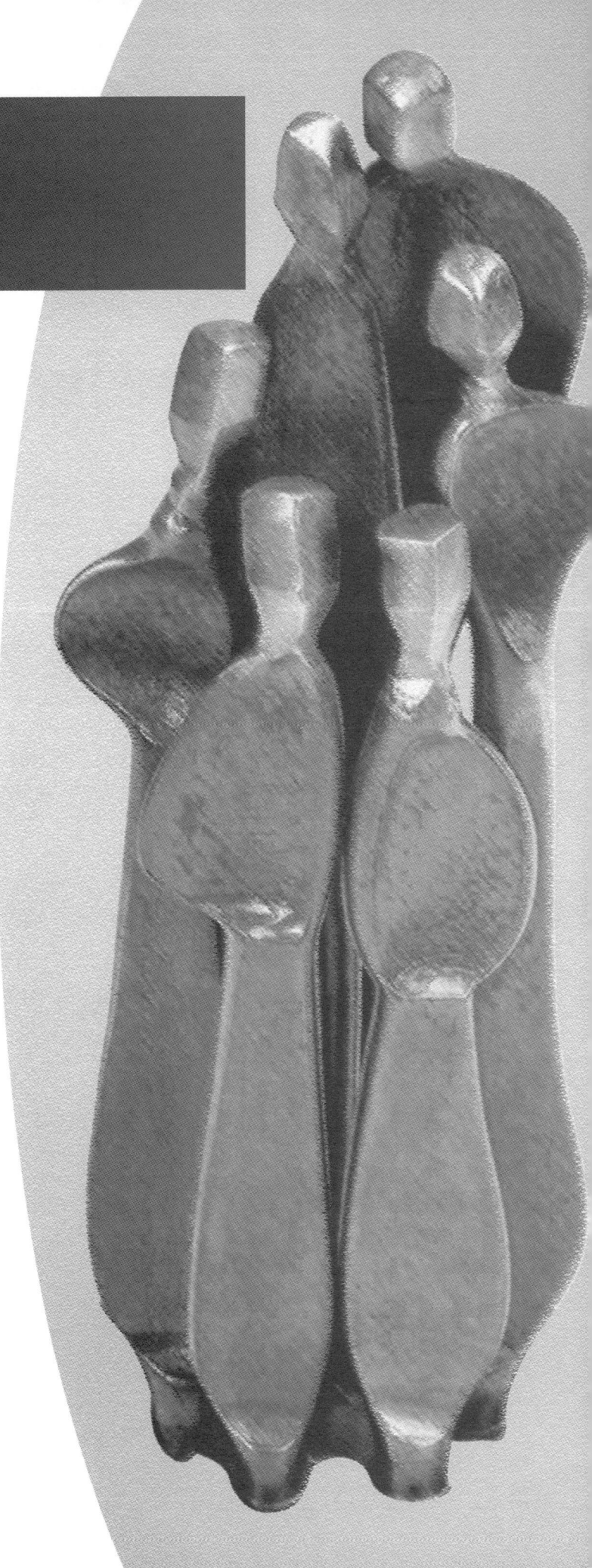

All Saints Day

WHAT IS A SAINT ANYWAY?

Focus: *To learn about saints of old and explore what it means to be a saint today.*

Scripture: Hebrews 12:1

INTRODUCTION TO THE THEME

Who is a saint?

You will need: plain paper plates, crayons or markers, craft sticks or tongue depressors, tape.

▶ The learners will make two-faced masks out of the paper plates, attaching a craft stick or tongue depressor at the base to hold it up to the face. Use the following steps to make the mask.

1. First make holes for the eyes. Begin with small holes and enlarge as needed.
2. Attach the craft stick or tongue depressor at the bottom with tape.
3. On one side, draw an unhappy face. On the other side, draw a happy face.

▶ Have the class divide into groups of 3-6. Include all members of a family unit in one group. (If you have a small group you may do this all together.) Ask them to share their masks with each other and tell how it feels to be sad and how it feels to be happy.

▶ Ask the following questions:
• What sort of decorations have you just seen around town? (Halloween decorations.)

- Although you knew they weren't real, how scary were they?
  - If they had been real, how would you have felt?

▶ Have everyone hold up the sad side of their masks and share the following information. **Say:**

Halloween started back many years ago, even before Jesus was born. People didn't know the cause of many things. They believed that the dead would harm them, and they thought that supernatural powers caused the many bad things that happened. They called those powers that they thought brought bad things, witches and ghosts and monsters. They chose a day before the cold of the winter set in to do things to please the bad spirits that they believed in. They did this so the bad spirits wouldn't hurt them during those months when there was less daylight and it was cold. Believing in this was sort of like having an unhappy mask on all of the time, because the powers they believed in brought unhappy things.

We can let God's love show through us to others.

▶ Ask them to turn their masks to the happy side, and then **say:**

When Jesus came, we learned that God is a loving God. Although the people still didn't understand why the bad things happened, they could wear a happy face because they knew that God would be with them and would love them no matter what happened. Later we learned a lot more about what caused the bad things to happen, and we are still learning about that today. But we can remember Jesus, and we can let God's love show through us to others. That doesn't mean that we won't have sad times. God understands about sad times. But that does mean that we can remember that God will help us through the bad times.

◗ Ask if anyone knows what today is. Then **say:**

> Halloween was the time that people celebrated the bad
> side of life. Today is the day we celebrate the happi-
> ness and joy that Jesus brings to life. We call it All
> Saints Day, and we remember people who have died
> and people who are alive today who love God. If you
> love God you are a saint! We're going to learn about
> some people who have died but who loved God very
> much when they were alive.

EXPERIENCING THE THEME

Learn about saints of the past

You will need: Copies of Handout #5 for each person or for each family, construction paper, large needles, yarn, scissors, hymnal

◗ Distribute Handout #5. Read the litany on the first page together.

◗ Divide into seven groups. Include all members of
a family unit in one group. (If your class is small,
use fewer groups and assign two "saints" to a
group.) Have construction paper, a large needle,
and yarn available for each group so that they
can make the handout pages into booklets as
they work.

◗ Assign each group one of the persons written
about in the handout. Ask that someone in the
group read the information and then the group is
to decide how to tell the whole class about that
person. They will also make booklets out of their
pages. To do this they will place the pages on top
of a piece of construction paper and fold them all
in half. On the fold line they will use a needle
and yarn to sew the pages together.

◗ Come together and ask the different groups to share their findings.

◗ Remind the learners that anyone who loves God is a saint. Ask each
person to introduce themselves as a saint in the following manner.
"I'm Saint _____ and I love God."

◗ Sing the hymn "Sing with All the Saints in Glory."

RESPONDING TO THE THEME

What do I do as a saint?

You will need: light-colored construction paper, pencils, markers, yarn, small stained glass image, candle, matches

▶ Light the candle. Remind the class that a candle helps you remember that God is among us. Set the candle aside. Hold up the stained glass image and **ask:**

What do you see?
What is it made of?
What is it used for?

▶ Hold the candle behind it and **ask:**

What happens when I hold the candle behind it?
How does it make the stained glass different?

> **Say: Saints are very much like the stained glass. They are people who love God so much that they allow God's light and love to shine through them. They make life more beautiful and help us to be closer to God.**

▶ Hand out construction paper and pencils. On one side of the paper, ask them to list different ways that they can show that they are saints, ways they can let the love of God shine through them.

▶ Ask each person to turn the construction paper over and make a nametag, using "Saint" with their name. Make two holes at the top of the paper and thread a piece of yarn through them and tie the ends in order to hang the name tag around the neck.

▶ Tell them to take the name tag home and use their list to remind them to act as a saint this week.

CELEBRATING THE THEME

Celebrate the saints

You will need: CD or cassette tape of marching music and player, hymnals, Bible

▶ Ask someone to read Hebrews 12:1.

> Saints are very much like the stained glass. They are people who love God so much that they allow God's light and love to shine through them.

- Stand and sing "Rise Up, O Men of God" but substitute the word "saints" for "men."

- Ask the class to imagine all of the Bible people who loved God marching in a parade. Then ask them to imagine all of the people of the church who lived long ago marching in the parade. Tell them that all of the people who have lived before us are something like a parade of saints marching down through the years.

- Read the following prayer, asking everyone to repeat each line after you. **Say:**

  > **Our God, we celebrate All Saints Day.**
  > **Many people in the past have loved you.**
  > **We have learned about your love from them.**
  > **We want to show our love for you too.**
  > **We want to be saints in your parade!**
  > **Amen.**

- Ask everyone to place their name tags over their heads for your march of the saints. They may use the happy side of their masks too, if they like.

- Play marching music on the CD or tape player. Invite the "saints" to march around the room, or in the hall.

- Consider having the class visit an adult class and share what they have learned about All Saints Day.

Ask the class to imagine all of the Bible people who loved God marching in a parade.

Ash Wednesday

[**Note**: There is another category for Lent. You may interchange these activities with those in the Lent category.]

Focus: *To recognize Ash Wednesday as the beginning of Lent.*

Scripture: Matthew 4:1-2; Luke 4:1-2

INTRODUCTION TO THE THEME

Plant seeds (bulbs may be substituted for seeds)

You will need: paper cups or small pots, potting soil, flower seeds or bulbs, hymnals, old newspaper or sheets

▶ Place newspaper or sheets on the working surface to protect it. Lay out the supplies.

▶ Invite learners to first write their names on their cup or pot and then plant seeds in them. As everyone works, talk about how the seeds look dead but there is really new life inside. Ask what the seeds require to grow and produce flowers.

▶ After the seeds have been planted, gather around the pots of seeds and ask if anyone knows what season you are beginning. Use the following information to explain Lent. **Say:**

> **The word "Lent" comes from an old Anglo-Saxon word** *lencten,* **which means springtime. The days are growing longer and the earth is beginning to prepare for new life. When we think of things growing, we think about how we grow closer to God.**
>
> **Lent is a forty-day period before Easter, not counting Sundays. The number of days in Lent is also the number of days that Jesus spent in the wilderness after his baptism. During Lent we try to grow closer to God. We remember things that we have done that keep us from being close to God. Some people call these sins. We ask God to forgive us of those sins. That is called**

The word "Lent" comes from an old Anglo-Saxon word *lencten,* which means springtime.

repentance. Lent also gives us time to remember Jesus' life and what happened just before he died and was raised from the dead.

Ash Wednesday is the first of the forty days. We call it Ash Wednesday because on that day we acknowledge ways that we have acted that are not as God would have us act, and we ask forgiveness for those times. We recognize that God takes those sins away, just like burning them up into ashes. Some churches have a special service on Ash Wednesday. During the service the pastor or priest uses ashes to make a cross on the foreheads of the worshipers.

▶ Sing or read "Hymn of Promise." This hymn is in many hymnals, but if you are not familiar with the tune, simply read the words. **Say:**

In the bulb there is a flower; in the seed, an apple tree;
in cocoons, a hidden promise: butterflies will soon be free.
In the cold and snow of winter there's a spring that waits to be,
unrevealed until its season, something God alone can see.

There's a song in every silence, seeking word and melody;
there's a dawn in every darkness, bringing hope to you and me.
From the past will come the future; what it holds, a mystery,
unrevealed until its season, something God alone can see.

In our end is our beginning; in our time, infinity;
in our doubt there is believing; in our life, eternity.
In our death, a resurrection; at the last, a victory,
*unrevealed until its season, something God alone can see.**

EXPERIENCING THE THEME

Learn about times of reflection

You will need: Bible

▶ Read Matthew 4:1-2 and Luke 4:1-2. Ask the learners what these scriptures tell us about Jesus. Ask them what the scripture sections have in common with what they have learned about Lent. Ask if there is a special place they like to go to when they want to pray or talk with God.

We recognize that God takes those sins away, just like burning them up into ashes. During the service the pastor or priest uses ashes to make a cross on the foreheads of the worshipers.

Make pretzels

You will need: pretzel ingredients, mixing bowl, measuring cups, measuring spoons, stirring spoon, greased baking sheet, toaster oven or access to regular stove, milk or juice (optional)

Pretzels (makes 15-20 pretzels)

1 pkg. dry yeast
1½ cups warm water
1 tablespoon sugar
1 teaspoon salt
4 cups flour
1 egg, beaten

Preheat oven to 425 degrees. Mix warm water, yeast, and sugar. Watch as it bubbles (about 5 minutes). Meanwhile mix salt and flour in a bowl. Add the yeast mixture. Turn out on floured surface and knead dough until smooth. Divide the dough into 20 portions. Roll each portion into a pencil thin roll and twist the dough according to the directions in picture. Place pretzels on greased baking sheet and brush with beaten egg. Bake for 12 minutes or until lightly brown.

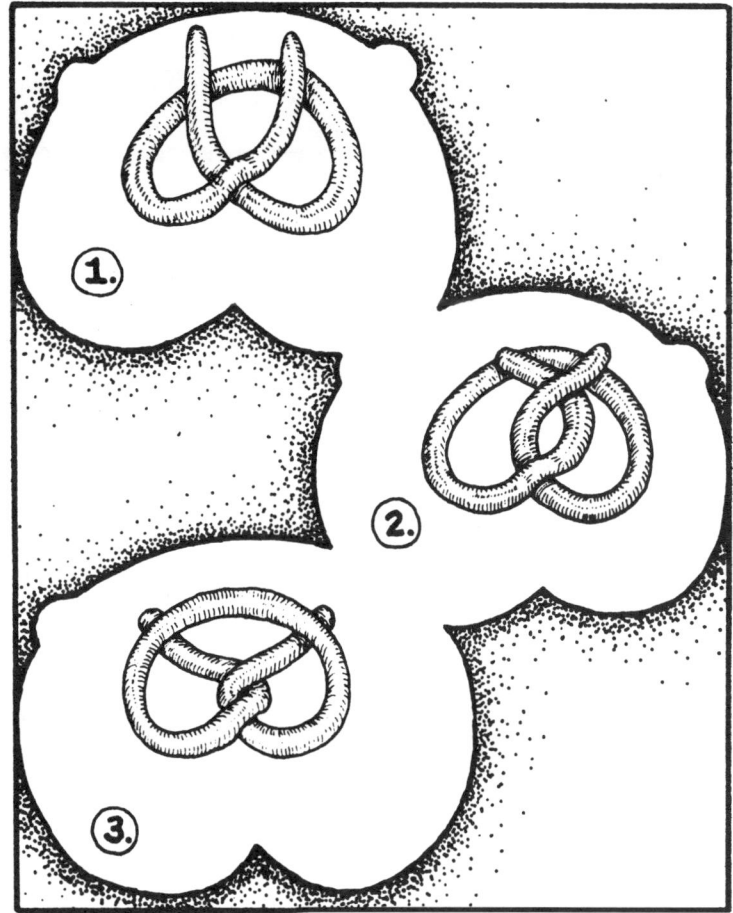

▶ As the pretzels are baking explain the origin and symbolism of the pretzels. **Say:**

> **Pretzels are symbolic of arms folded in prayer and are believed to have come from the fifth century when the Christians in Rome remembered Jesus praying in the garden. The Latin name for the bread, *bracellae*, means "little arms." As the custom left Rome and moved into central and northern Europe the word became *bratzel* and later *pretzel*. The Sunday after Ash Wednesday is sometimes called Pretzel Sunday. This reminded the people that Lent was a time for prayer. In the past pretzels were never eaten after Palm Sunday, but today we eat them year round.**

▶ Pray this special prayer and then enjoy the pretzels. You may want to add milk or juice to your treat. **Say:**

> **We ask you to bless this special Lenten bread, O Lord. Help us to use the folded arms to remind us of your**

Pretzels are symbolic of arms folded in prayer and are believed to have come from the fifth century.

love and how your love holds us. As we pray during Lent, may we remember Jesus and all he did for us. Amen.

RESPONDING TO THE THEME

Make crosses of nails

You will need: two large square nails for each person, purple yarn, sample cross

▶ Place two nails in a crossed fashion. Using one end of the yarn, bind the nails together. The remainder of the yarn can be made into a "chain" to wear around the neck.

▶ **Ask: Why do we use the cross as a symbol? What do the nails remind you of?**

▶ Suggest that the learners use the cross during Lent to remember the suffering of Jesus that turned into joy.

Make Lenten palm branch

You will need: copies of Handout #8 for each participant, green construction paper, scissors, glue or tape.

▶ Each learner will begin the palm branch and add to it each day during Lent using the instructions on Handout #8. Read the John 3:16 passage and then have everyone tape that palm frond to their branch. If several days have passed since Ash Wednesday, tell them that they can add the palm fronds for the days gone by at any time during Lent by simply doing as the handout suggests and adding the fronds. Ask each learner to take their remaining palm fronds home and add one each day, following the directions on the handout for each day during Lent.

CELEBRATING THE THEME

You will need: note pad sized paper, pencils, large pan or metal pail that can be used for burning paper, matches

▶ Ask learners to tell of something that they have learned about Ash Wednesday and Lent.

▶ Summarize with two main parts of Lent: *remembering Jesus and what he taught us;* and *recognizing things we are doing that keep us from showing our love for God and asking God's forgiveness for those things.*

Part II: Planned Sessions

Say: When we don't act the way that we should to other people, or when we forget to love God, God has a sad heart. God loves with a happy heart and God loves with a sad heart, but God always loves. We can never do anything that will cause God not to love us.

▶ Give paper and pencils to learners and ask them to write at least one thing on the paper that they have done in the past that they think may have caused God to have a sad heart. Tell them that this is private and no one will see what they have written. Young children may draw a picture instead of writing.

▶ After they have completed it, ask them to fold the paper and hold it as you pray. **Say:**

> **Our Loving God, we remember times when we have not done as you would have us do. We remember times when we've forgotten about your love. We ask your forgiveness. (Pause) Now we know that we are forgiven. Thank you for forgiving us. Amen.**

▶ Ask the learners to crumple their papers and place them in the pan or pail.

▶ Sing the doxology, "Praise God from Whom All Blessings Flow."

▶ Move outside and burn the paper into ashes. Tell the learners that you will spread the ashes on a garden (or share any other plan you have for their disposal).

NOTE: You may use a paper shredder to destroy the papers. These then may be put into a compost bin to be recycled into dirt.

Celebrating Advent 1

WHAT IS ADVENT?

Focus: *To explore the meaning of Advent and consider ways to celebrate Christ's coming.*

Scripture: Isaiah 11:1-2*a*

INTRODUCTION TO THE THEME

Drawing a waiting time

You will need: drawing paper, crayons or markers

▶ Invite learners to draw pictures of times they have had to wait for something.

▶ Bring learners together and invite each person to give his or her name and tell about the drawing.

▶ **Ask: When we are expecting these things to happen, how can we get ready for it to come about?**
- **A move to a new home**
- **The birth of a baby**
- **The beginning of school**
- **A vacation trip**
- **The visit of a grandparent or other guest**
- **A picnic**

▶ **Say: When we prepare for anything, we must know something about what we are preparing for. Advent is a time that we prepare to celebrate the birth of Jesus, whom we also call Christ. The church prepares in several ways.** (List some of the things that you do in your church during Advent such as hanging banners, lighting an Advent wreath, and decorating the sanctuary and other areas.)

- **Ask: What are some ways that we can prepare our homes?** (They may give suggestions such as cleaning our houses, decorating, writing letters to friends, preparing food, and reading the Christmas story.)

- **Ask: What are some things we can do to prepare ourselves?** (They may give suggestions such as remembering things we have done that are not nice and asking God to forgive us, learning more about God, reading about Jesus, and praying.)

EXPERIENCING THE THEME

Explore announcements

You will need: a variety of announcements of upcoming events, such as bulletin notices, invitations, and newspaper articles or ads

- Divide the class into groups, depending on the number of announcements you brought. Include all members of a family unit in one group. Ask the groups to read their announcement and be prepared to summarize what the announcement is about. Ask each group to share their findings with the class.

- **Say: There is an announcement in our Bible that tells about the coming of Christ. Listen while it is read.**

- Ask someone to read Isaiah 11:1-2*a*.

RESPONDING TO THE THEME

Make an Advent Wreath

You will need: circular foam base for each household, knife, four purple and one white candles for each household, evergreens, candleholder, Handout #2

- Each family or household will make a wreath, using a circular foam base. Cut holes for candles in the wreath at four even spaces around the circle. Place four purple candles in the holes. Cover the base with evergreens. Give each household a white candle to be placed in a candle holder in the center of the wreath. Each family will also receive Handout #2 with the instructions on page 131.

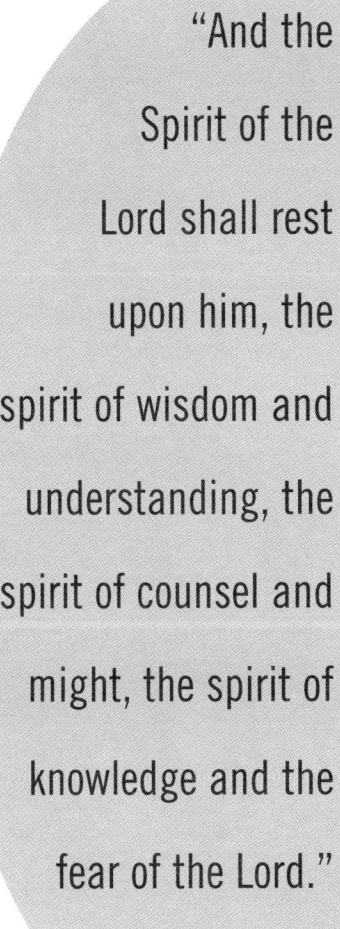

"And the Spirit of the Lord shall rest upon him, the spirit of wisdom and understanding, the spirit of counsel and might, the spirit of knowledge and the fear of the Lord."

— Isaiah 11:2 (RSV)

AND/OR

Make an Advent Chain

NOTE: If you are short of time, this may be made at home, taping the chain together as a link is read each day.

You will need: copies of Handout #1 for each participant, scissors, glue or tape.

▶ **Say: We prepare for an event by learning something about it or something about the person being celebrated. During Advent we can prepare to celebrate Christmas by learning more about Jesus.**

▶ Each family will make an Advent chain using Handout #1, scissors and glue or tape. The links should be made with the printing on the outside so that each message can be read. Families will take the chain home and read and follow the directions on the designated link of the chain each day between now and Christmas. They may even want to use the chain as holiday decoration in their home.

CELEBRATING THE THEME

You will need: hymnal, Advent wreath, chalkboard or newsprint and marker, matches.

▶ Use the class Advent wreath and light the first candle. Read Isaiah 11:1-2*a* again.

▶ Create a litany by asking the learners to think of one way that we prepare for Christmas. List these on the chalkboard or newsprint, asking each person to remember what he or she suggested. After several suggestions have been made, say that you have just created a litany. You will begin with one sentence, and then when you point to one of the statements on the chalkboard or newsprint, the person who suggested it will read it. After each one, the class will respond with, "We prepare for Christmas." Begin the litany using words such as these. **Say:**

> **Our God, we came together today to consider Advent and all that it means to us. Advent is our time to prepare for the celebration of when Christ came as a small baby to be among us.** (At this time, point to the first statement and after it is read lead the group in the response, **"We prepare for Christmas."**) Close with Amen.

▶ Ask everyone to sing "O Come, O Come, Emmanuel" as you close the session.

Advent is our time to prepare for the celebration of when Christ came as a small baby to be among us.

Celebrating Advent 2

Focus: *To explore the meaning of some of our Advent and Christmas symbols.*

Scripture: Matthew 2:9-10; 3:16
Luke 2:6-9; 19:37-38
John 1:29; 3:16; 8:12

INTRODUCTION TO THE THEME

Write picture poem

You will need: paper, pencils, symbol stencils (see Handout #3)

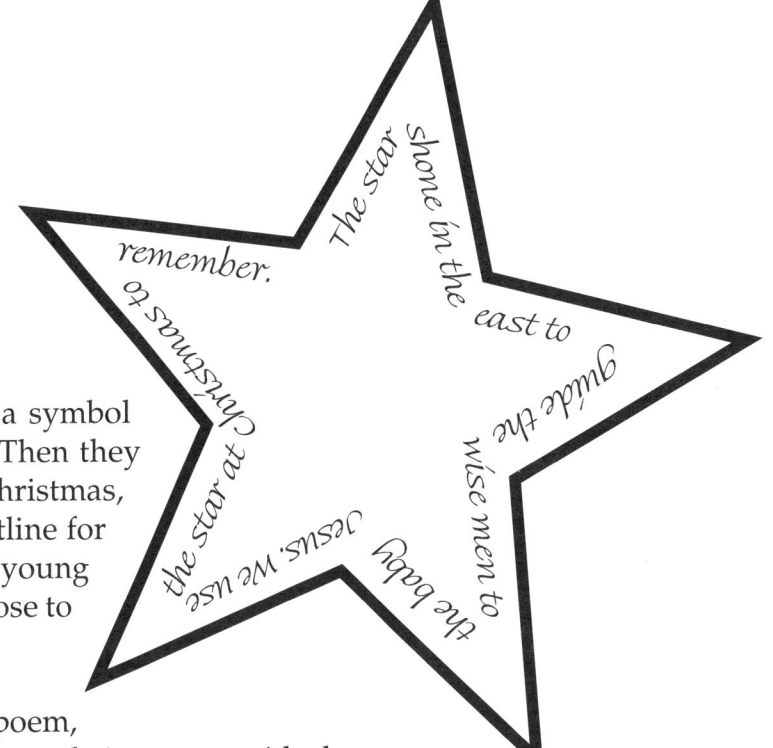

▶ As the learners enter, ask them to select a symbol stencil and draw the outline on a paper. Then they will write a sentence or two about Christmas, using the outline of the symbol as the outline for their writing. Parents will need to help young children with this. Early arrivers may choose to make several.

▶ When each person has made a picture poem, come together and ask the learners to share their poems with the class.

EXPERIENCING THE THEME

Make symbols

You will need: symbol stencils (see Handout #3), Bibles, light colored construction paper, pencils, hole punch, ribbon, crayons (glitter is optional)

Side by Side

▶ Set up eight activity stations. These may be separate tables, or you may have two stations to a table. You may also place the materials on the floor and have the learners sit on the floor to work. Place the construction paper, hole punch, and ribbon at a central location. At each station put a Bible and one of the following stencils with the accompanying scripture passage.

Star	**Matthew 2:9-10**
Manger	**Luke 2:6-7**
Angel	**Luke 2:9**
Lamb	**John 1:29, Luke 2:8**
Wreath	**John 3:16**
Crown	**Luke 19:37-38**
Candle	**John 8:12**
Dove	**Matthew 3:16**

▶ Give the following instructions. **Say: There are eight stations where you may work today. Move about as you like, but try to visit each station. At each station, read the assigned scripture verses and then draw the symbol. Talk about how the symbol reminds you of the scripture. At the central location we have construction paper, pencils, a hole punch, and ribbon for hanging the symbols. There are also crayons if you finish ahead of the others and would like to decorate your symbols.**

OR

Draw symbols

You will need: Bible, paper, crayons or markers, pictures of symbols

▶ Learners may sit at tables, work on the floor, or you may provide clipboards for their use. Tell them that you will read a scripture and they are to "doodle" or draw any pictures or symbols that come to mind as they listen. They may place their drawings anywhere on the page, turning the paper in any direction they like as they fill up all the blank spaces.

▶ Read the following verses, pausing between each scripture to discuss what the learners have drawn and to hold up the picture of the symbol that you have brought into the classroom. Affirm any drawings of other symbols or pictures that the learners have drawn. Remind them that one type of symbol may help one person recall a scripture, while another may be more helpful for someone else. With each scripture, ask if anyone can think of another symbol that could be used.

Matthew 2:9-10	Star
Luke 2:6-7	Manger
Luke 2:9	Angel
John 1:29, Luke 2:8	Lamb
John 3:16	Wreath
Luke 19:37-38	Crown
John 8:12	Candle
Matthew 3:16	Dove

RESPONDING TO THE THEME

Discuss symbols

You will need: chalkboard or newsprint and markers

▶ Tell the learners that we have many symbols and stories that we enjoy around Christmas. Some of the stories are true and some of them are might-have-been stories. Some have to do with the birth of Christ and some have been added to our tradition over the years, just for fun.

▶ Tell the story of St. Nicholas. **Say:**
About three hundred years after Jesus was born, there was another baby born in Italy, a country not too far from Jesus' country. His name was Nicholas. Young Nicholas loved to hear the stories about Jesus, especially the ones that told how Jesus loved everyone, even those who were poor and needy. When Nicholas became a man, he enjoyed giving gifts to others, but he would do it secretly, in the middle of the night, because he didn't want people to know where the gifts came from. In particular he gave gifts to the people who had very little.

One day he heard of a kind man who had three lovely daughters. Each of the daughters loved a young man and wanted to marry him, but in those days a girl had to have money, or a "dowry," before they could announce the wedding. The father was very poor and could not afford a "dowry." One daughter planned to sell herself as a slave so that the other two could marry.

About three hundred years after Jesus was born, there was another baby born in Italy, a country not too far from Jesus' country. His name was Nicholas. When Nicholas became a man, he enjoyed giving gifts to others, but he would do it secretly, in the middle of the night, because he didn't want people to know where the gifts came from.

When Nicholas heard of this, he took some of his money and put it in a bag. When it was dark he walked to their house. A window was open, and so he threw the money into the oldest girl's room. The girl had hung her stockings near the window to dry, and the money fell into the stocking. The girl had a marvelous wedding!

Later Nicholas did the same thing for the second daughter. That daughter also had a great wedding. But everyone wondered who was being so kind. There was only one daughter left. Would she also be so fortunate?

When Nicholas slipped into the house at night and left the money for the third daughter, the father caught him. Nicholas asked the father not to tell anyone who had done it, and the father kept the secret for many years.

Nicholas continued to help people without looking for thanks. He loved Jesus so much that he became a bishop in the church. Even when he was thrown into jail for being a Christian, he still shared God's love with others.

After he died they called him a saint. A saint is someone who loves God very much. We are all saints when we love God. As the years went by, people remembered St. Nicholas and how he gave gifts in secret. In Holland they call him *Sinterclaas*, in France he is called *Père Nöel*, in England they call him *Father Christmas*, in Brazil they call him *Pape Noel*, and in the United States we call him *Santa Claus*.

Whether the story about the sisters is true or not, we cannot be sure. But we do know that there was a man who became known as St. Nicholas who made a practice of giving gifts in secret because he loved Jesus so much.

▶ On the chalkboard or newsprint, make two columns. Title them **Christian symbols** and **commonplace symbols**.

▶ Under the Christian symbols column list the symbols you have worked with. Ask if anyone would like to share some new idea or insight that they have received about these symbols as they have worked with them.

We do know that there was a man who became known as St. Nicholas who made a practice of giving gifts in secret because he loved Jesus so much.

▶ Ask for other symbols that we use at Christmas. Before you list them, ask the group to decide under which column you should place them in and why. Talk about what each symbol stands for and whether it is something that specifically speaks of the real meaning of Christmas or just something we have added to our customs for the fun of it.

CELEBRATING THE THEME

You will need: Advent wreath, Bibles, hymnals, matches

▶ Tell the learners that you will make living symbols of the Christmas story. Divide the learners into three groups. Include all members of a family unit in one group. Assign the scriptures below to the groups and ask them to decide on a way that they can place their bodies in sculpture-like positions to represent the scenes from the story. They may use any props that they find around the room, but they may not move or speak once they are in position.

> Luke 2:6-7
> Luke 2:8-9
> Matthew 2:11

▶ After the groups have had time to decide what they will do, call on group 1 to get into position and then read the scripture. Then ask group 2 to get into position and read the scripture. And then have group 3 move into position and read the scripture.

▶ Sing the first verse of "Joy to the World."

▶ Close with this prayer which you will line out and they will repeat. **Say:**

> **Thank you, God, for sending Jesus.**
> **We know that Jesus taught us to give to others.**
> **Help us to remember just why we give at Christmas.**
> **Amen.**

We know that Jesus taught us to give to others. Help us to remember just why we give at Christmas.

Celebrating Advent 3

CHRISTMAS CAROLS

Focus: *To learn the story behind some of our Christmas carols.*

Scripture: Isaiah 11:1-3; Luke 2:1-20; 2 Corinthians 5:19; Matthew 2:1-12; Psalm 98:4-9

INTRODUCTION TO THE THEME

Draw a picture

You will need: paper, crayons or markers

▶ As each learner enters, invite him or her to draw a picture that describes a favorite Christmas carol or song about Jesus' birth. Ask them to label their pictures.

▶ Ask class members to explain their pictures and then display them at your gathering spot.

How carols began

▶ Tell the learners the following information about the beginning of singing during worship and how Christmas carols began. **Say:**

> The earlier religious songs that are recorded are in the Old Testament. In fact, the oldest parts of the Scripture that we know of were actually words to songs that were sung by Miriam, the sister of Moses (Exodus 15:1-21) and Deborah, one of the judges of early Israel (Judges 4, 5). Choirs of both men and women continued to sing through the centuries, even into the first centuries of Christianity. However, when Christianity became legalized and institutionalized in the fourth

Choirs of both men and women continued to sing through the centuries, even into the first centuries of Christianity.

century, women were pushed out of leadership. In fact, there was very little congregational singing. Most of the music was sung by professional choirs of men and boys. When women's convents were established, the women sang in their own areas and a few even wrote music. But it was not until the Protestant Reformation that the general congregational singing came back into worship.

The origin of the term Christmas carol is up for debate. The word "carol" may be traced back to the Greek word *choros* which means a dance. The word *choraules* means a person who accompanies a dance. In early Greek culture these dances were circle dances for festive occasions. They were used with the early plays that told the story of Jesus' birth. During medieval times, St. Francis of Assisi wanted the common people to understand the story of Jesus' birth, and so he set up a manger with a doll in it in the church sanctuary so that the whole congregation could see it. The children brought gifts and created songs and dances for the Christ Child. Our small manger scenes had their beginnings here. As the custom of setting up these scenes spread, people began singing special Christmas songs around them, sometimes accompanied by dance. These became known as Christmas carols. The carols are joyful and tell about the glad news of Christ's birth.

> The carols are joyful and tell about the glad news of Christ's birth.

EXPERIENCING THE THEME

Explore the stories behind the carols

You will need: Copies of the stories in Handout #4, hymnals, dictionaries

▶ Decide ahead of time how many carols you will use and divide the class into that number of groups. Include all members of a family unit in one group. If you have a small class and ample time, you might choose to give each group two carols to work with.

▶ The groups will read the material about the background of the carol. Then they will read the verses of the carol and explore the meaning of any words they do not understand. Tell them that you have dictionaries if they want to look up any words. They will prepare and share their findings with the whole class.

RESPONDING TO THE THEME

Make plans for caroling

▶ There are many people who are lonely at Christmastime for a variety of reasons. Some may be in nursing homes or hospitals. Decide on a time when your class can visit and sing Christmas carols for them. If you would like to take some cookies or other treats along, either plan for everyone to bring them or arrange to bake them before your visit. You may also want to plan a fun gathering afterward with hot cocoa and games.

OR

Write a carol

You will need: chalkboard or newsprint and marker

▶ Use the tune of a familiar carol and create different words by using the following steps:

1. Decide on a theme. Will you tell part of the story in the carol? Will you sing about the joy or happiness over the good news of Jesus' birth? Will you sing about praising God? Write the theme on the chalkboard or newsprint.
2. Ask for words or phrases that describe the theme. Write these on the chalkboard or newsprint in no particular order.
3. Decide on a tune. This may be the tune of a carol or it may be another common tune, such as "Row, Row, Row Your Boat."
4. Choose the words or phrases from your list and put them into the tune, adding and changing the words as necessary. Try singing the tune with several different phrases until you come to an agreement.
5. Write the words on another sheet of newsprint or in another area of the chalkboard.

CELEBRATING THE THEME

You will need: Advent wreath, matches, hymnals

▶ Assign reading parts for the following introductions to the carols. If you did not study all of the carols or do not plan to use all of the songs for this celebration, only hand out those you will use.

"O Come, O Come, Emmanuel"—This carol has come down to us through the centuries, being adjusted and adapted at various times.

> "O Come, O Come, Emmanuel" has come down to us through the centuries, being adjusted and adapted at various times.

But it still gives us great joy to sing it when we prepare ourselves for Christmas.

"O Little Town of Bethlehem"—The words of this carol remind us of the ordinary world that Jesus came to with an extraordinary message.

"Silent Night, Holy Night"—This carol has become one of the most loved carols in the world, and as Franz Gruber's wife said, "We will die, you and I, but this song will live."

"Away in a Manger"—The words of this song bring to our minds just what it may have been like on that night over 2,000 years ago when Jesus was born.

"Hark! the Herald Angels Sing"—This carol not only tells the story of the shepherds' encounter with the angels, but brings deep understanding of Christian spirituality.

"Go, Tell It on the Mountain"—In this song Christians are called to proclaim this special birth of a Savior from the highest point of the mountain.

"We Three Kings"—This carol helps us to tell the story according to Matthew's Gospel.

"Joy to the World"—This song expresses praise of Jesus Christ in unsurpassed joy. We cannot help expressing that joy as we sing it.

▶ Light three candles on the Advent wreath.

▶ Ask the assigned readers to read their introductions just before you sing the first verse of each carol.

▶ Close by using verse four of "O Little Town of Bethlehem" as a prayer.

> The words of "Away in a Manger" bring to our minds just what it may have been like on that night over 2,000 years ago when Jesus was born.

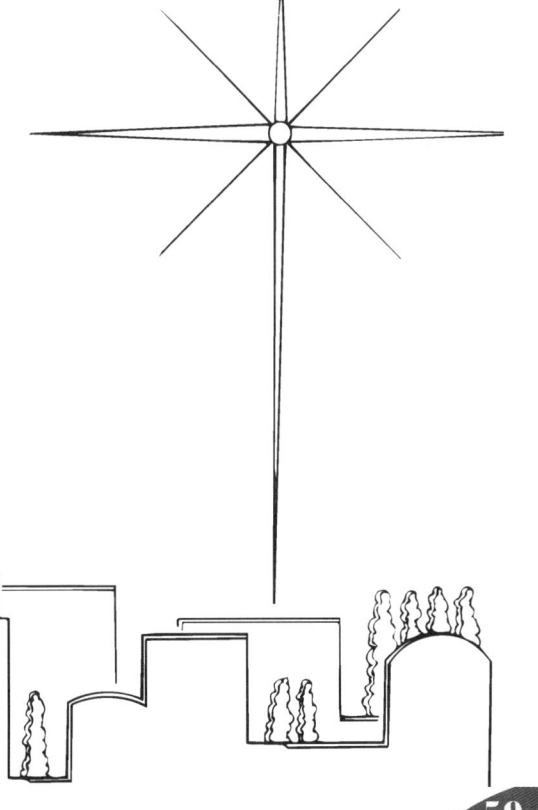

Celebrating Advent 4

WHAT REALLY HAPPENED?

Focus: *To explore the situation of Jesus' birth.*

Scripture: Luke 2:1-7

INTRODUCTION TO THE THEME

Compare baby situations then and now

You will need: various baby items, such as diapers, blankets, baby bottles, baby shampoo, and so on. Try to also include some things that are not common.

▶ As the learners arrive, ask them to look over the assortment of baby items that you have displayed and see if they can identify just what purpose each item has.

▶ When everyone has had an opportunity to look at the baby items, explain that today as you prepare for Christmas you will look at what life was like when Jesus was born.

▶ As you pick up each item ask persons to explain its use and whether such an item might have been used when Jesus was a baby.

▶ Ask what other things might have been different about the birth of Jesus and the birth of a baby today. (They might suggest hospitals, doctors, medicines, nice baby beds, incubators, and so on.)

EXPERIENCING THE THEME

Answer the questions

You will need: a large sign that says "true" and another that says "false" (If space is a problem, this may be done by having the learners answer true or false on a piece of paper.)

▶ Tell the class that sometimes we get the Christmas story a little confused because of the way that stores and other businesses present the story. Read the following versions of the Christmas story and ask the learners to listen carefully to the details.

> **Luke 2:1-20**
> **Matthew 2:1-15**

▶ Tell the learners that you will read several sentences and they are to move to the sign that says "true" if they believe the statement is true, or move to the sign that says "false" if they believe it is untrue. If the scripture doesn't tell us one way or the other, they are to move to the "false" sign.

▶ Read the following statements, give the learners time to move to one of the signs, and then read the answer. Say:

> 1. Mary rode a donkey to Bethlehem.
> *Answer: Their transportation is not mentioned in the scriptures.*
>
> 2. The stable had cows and donkeys in it.
> *Answer: The scriptures do not tell us.*
>
> 3. The angels sang their message to the shepherds
> *Answer: The scriptures say ". . . praising God and saying, 'Glory to God. . . .' "*
>
> 4. There were three wise men.
> *Answer: The scriptures mention three gifts, but the number of wise men is not given.*
>
> 5. The star that guided the wise men was seen in the east.
> *Answer: According to the scriptures, the wise men came from the east, and the star guided them to Bethlehem. Some translations say that they saw the star in the east, which could mean they saw the star when they were in the east. Some translations say they saw the star ". . . at its rising."*
>
> 6. The wise men rode camels.
> *Answer: There is no mention of the transportation of the wise men.*
>
> 7. The wise men were kings.
> *Answer: They are only called "wise men" in the scripture.*
>
> 8. The wise men first looked for Jesus in Bethlehem.
> *Answer: They first looked for Jesus in Jerusalem, questioning King Herod.*

According to the scriptures, the wise men came from the east, and the star guided them to Bethlehem.

9. The wise men found Jesus in a manger in Bethlehem.
Answer: The scripture says: "On entering the house, they saw the child. . . ."

10. Mary and Joseph rode a donkey to Egypt.
Answer: We are not told what mode of travel they used to leave the country.

RESPONDING TO THE THEME

Make a manger scene

You will need: commercial clay or corn starch/salt clay using the recipe below.

½ cup corn starch	¾ cup water
1 cup salt	paints

Mix the corn starch, salt, and water. Place this in the top of a double boiler and heat, stirring until it is difficult to stir. Spoon mixture onto wax paper to cool and then knead it until it is smooth and there is no air in it. Store the mixture in a plastic bag until you are ready to shape the figures. After the figures are formed, allow them to dry before painting them. Each recipe makes three 3-inch figures.

Give each family unit enough clay to make at least three figures. Suggest that they make the body of each figure from a cylinder of about ¾ inch across and 2-3 inches long. A small ball can be placed on top to form the head.

AND/OR

Draw an "icon"

You will need: legal size paper, crayons or markers

▶ Explain that years ago most people could not read the Bible stories themselves, so churches created stained glass windows or pictures, called icons, to help them remember the story. Use a legal size paper and fold it into thirds. On the center third draw a picture of Mary, Joseph, and the baby in the manger. On the left third, draw the shepherds and the angel. On the right third, draw the wise men. Stand the paper vertically to make it an icon.

CELEBRATING THE THEME

Tell the story in song

You will need: Advent wreath, matches, nativity figures, hymnals

▶ Ask class members to help you decide just how to set up the manger (nativity) figures. Remind them of what they learned concerning what really happened according to the scripture.

▶ Light all four candles of the Advent wreath.

▶ Sing the following carols, which tell the story of Jesus' birth. Ask learners to pay attention to the wording in particular songs that might not be completely accurate according to what they learned earlier in this session.

"O Little Town of Bethlehem" (verse 1)
"Away in a Manger" (verse 1)
"While Shepherds Watched Their Flocks" (verse 1)
"Silent Night, Holy Night" (verse 1)
"We Three Kings" (verse 1)
"Joy to the World" (verse 1)

▶ Close with a prayer something like this:

We thank you, God, for that night long ago when Jesus was born. We remember it today, even though we don't know everything about how it happened. We do know that you sent Jesus to help us learn how to be closer to you. Thank you for Jesus. Amen.

"We thank you, God, for that night long ago when Jesus was born."

God's Gift of Friendship

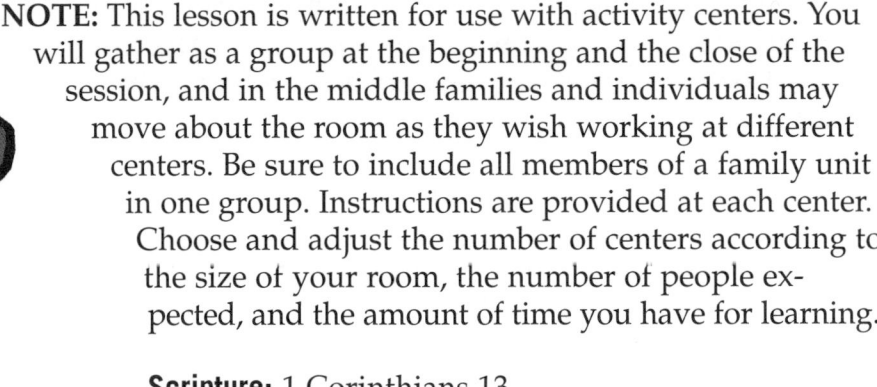

Focus: *To explore various types of friendship and what it means to be a friend.*

[**NOTE:** This lesson is written for use with activity centers. You will gather as a group at the beginning and the close of the session, and in the middle families and individuals may move about the room as they wish working at different centers. Be sure to include all members of a family unit in one group. Instructions are provided at each center. Choose and adjust the number of centers according to the size of your room, the number of people expected, and the amount of time you have for learning.]

Scripture: 1 Corinthians 13

INTRODUCTION TO THE THEME

Draw on Friendship Graffiti Wall

You will need: shelf paper or sheets or a roll of newsprint, colored washable markers

▶ Attach the paper to the wall (Note: Test the paper to see if it bleeds through to the wall. If so, use additional layers to protect the wall.) Label the paper: **Friendship Graffiti Wall**

▶ As the learners enter, ask each person to write words or phrases, or draw pictures about friendship.

Discuss friendship

▶ Come together and view the graffiti wall. Affirm the different statements and pictures.

▶ Share with the learners the following information about different types of friendship: *close friends*, *good friends*, and *casual friends*. **Say:**

> *Close friends*—**In our lifetime we may have only two or three friends we can actually call close. A common**

feeling and understanding flows between close friends. They can reveal things to each other that might hurt other types of friendships.

Good friends—These friends are more prevalent, and the relationship offers great rewards. Good friends enjoy many things in common. They thrive on the give-and-take of conversations on mutual interests. They share their excitement and joys as well as their sorrows. A good friend may develop into a close friend, given the right circumstances.

Casual friends—We have many casual friends. They develop with neighborhood interaction, business associates, and through other friends. They are the wildflower garden of life; growth depends on the location and climate. They may become good or close friends.[*]

EXPERIENCING AND RESPONDING TO THE THEME

[**NOTE:** To prepare for this part of the session, set up various centers around the room. These may be on tables, on the floor, or even on the wall. Instructions for set-up are listed below. See Handout #6 "Friendship" for the instructions for use of the centers. Cut apart one copy of the handout and mount the appropriate instructions at each activity center. Next, delete the centers that you don't plan to use from the handout, and create a sheet with only the centers you will set up. Make copies of your revised version of handout #6 for each family unit to use as they visit the centers.]

▶ Tell the learners that they will have _____ amount of time to work with the centers around the room. Help them divide into groups. Include all members of a family unit in one group. Tell them that they will not have time to visit all of the centers so they must choose the ones they want to visit. Distribute copies of your revised version of Handout #6. Tell everyone that you will give a two-minute warn-

A common feeling and understanding flows between close friends. They can reveal things to each other that might hurt other types of friendships.

[*] "My Friends: Who Are They?" by Delia Halverson. *The Church School,* May 1978 issue, page 28, Cokesbury.

ing before time to come back together. Use the following information to set up the desired learning centers:

Mobiles—Place at this center: paper, crayons or markers, 1/4 inch doweling or small sticks, string, hole punch, scissors

Crossword Hopscotch—This center can be created in two ways. Either draw the hopscotch on a sidewalk outside or use masking tape on the floor to create the hopscotch. Inside each square write different friendship words, such as: *trusting, alike, different, free, loyal, unselfish, sharing, laughter, forgiveness*. Provide flat stones for playing the game.

Write a Friend—Place at this center: note paper, envelopes, and pens and pencils

Friendship Banner—Place at this center: posterboard or rolls of shelf paper and markers. If you like, you can use fabric, lace, and other sewing items and the banners may be glued or sewn together.

Make a Collage—Place at this center: magazines, poster board, scissors, and glue. Label the poster board "Friendship Is . . ."

Rock Painting—Place at this center: flat rocks, acrylic paints, brushes, water and paper towels for clean-up. Be sure to protect the working surface with old newspapers or cloth.

Bumper Sticker—Place at this center: strips of legal size paper cut lengthwise (4 1/4 x 13 1/2") and clear contact paper cut two inches larger than the paper all around (8 1/4 x 17 1/2"), permanent markers, Bible.

Read Bible Stories—Place at this center: Bible

Cycle of Friendship—Place at this center: large sheets of paper, pencils, crayons

Build a Neighborhood—Place at this center: building blocks, play cars and people

Paint a Friendship Picture—Place at this center: tempera paints, brushes, paper, painting smocks, water and towels for clean-up. Easels may also be used, if they are available.

Paraphrase Scripture—Place at this center: Bible, paper, pencils

Act as Reporter—Place at this center: audio or video recorder and tape

Take a Picture—Place at this center: Polaroid camera and film, pen

CELEBRATING THE THEME

You will need: hymnals

▶ Call the groups together. (Be sure to give them a two-minute warning so that they can finish up at the center where they are working.)

▶ Ask groups to share something about their experiences during the session.

▶ Ask persons to mention words about friendship at the appropriate time during the following prayer. **Say:**

> **Our God, who is also a friend, we thank you for friendship.**
>
> **We learned that good friends are: (allow persons to mention words about friendship)**
>
> **We know that good friendship binds or ties us all together.**
>
> **Thank you for all of our friends here and our friends in other places.**
> **Amen.**

▶ Sing together "Blest Be the Tie That Binds."

We know that good friendship binds or ties us all together.

Pentecost: The Birthday of the Church

Focus: *To reflect on Pentecost and the birthday of the church.*

Scripture: Acts 2:1-8; 12-18; 44-47

INTRODUCTION TO THE THEME

Draw on Church Graffiti Wall

You will need: shelf paper, or sheets or a roll of newsprint, colored washable markers.

▶ Attach the paper to the wall. Test the paper to see if it bleeds through to the wall. If so, use additional layers as protection. Label the paper: **Our Church**

▶ As the learners enter, ask each person to write words or phrases or draw some picture about what they like best about their church.

▶ After all have finished, gather around the wall and ask each person to explain their words or pictures.

▶ Sing together "We Are the Church."

EXPERIENCING THE THEME

Explore birthdays

You will need: photos of birthdays. (Prior to the lesson, ask families to bring photos of memorable birthdays to share. Bring a few yourself.)

▶ Ask families to share various ways that they celebrate birthdays. Comment on how some families celebrate in similar fashions, while others have special ways to celebrate.

▶ Share the photos of birthdays that were brought by various families.

▶ Ask if anyone can guess the connection between the church and celebration of birthdays. Explain that you are celebrating Pentecost, or the celebration of when the followers of Jesus really became a church.

Tell the story

You will need: Bible, 3 pieces of poster board (each cut in half), crayons or markers, Handout #9

▶ **Say: Pentecost occurs fifty days after Easter and marks the gift of the Holy Spirit to Jesus' followers. Israel celebrated Pentecost long before the time of Christ. If was also called the Feast of Weeks, a celebration after the first fruits were gathered. Bread was made from freshly harvested grain and offered as a sacrifice to God.**

▶ Divide the class into six groups. Include all members of a family unit in one group. (If you have smaller numbers, use fewer groups and assign the additional symbols as needed.) Give each group one of the symbols and the accompanying information from Handout #9. Each group will draw the symbol they are assigned and be prepared to read the explanation to the class.

▶ After the posters are finished, explain the following about symbols. **Say:**

> **In the early years of Christianity, when there was fear of being killed because of your beliefs, symbols were used to keep their Christian identity a secret. Symbols were a test of identity among the Christians themselves. Symbols were later used to tell a story to those who could not read, reminding them of a familiar story.**

▶ After the posters are made, come together in a large group. Have someone read Acts 2:1-8 and then ask the group members with Pentecost symbols of the *wind, flame,* and *three interwoven circles (Trinity)* to hold up their posters and explain them.

▶ Have someone read Acts 2:12-18; 44-47 and then ask the group members with early church symbols of the *torch, fish,* and *monogram* to hold up their posters and explain them.

In the early years of Christianity, when there was fear of being killed because of your beliefs, symbols were used to keep their Christian identity a secret.

RESPONDING TO THE THEME

NOTE: For this theme I have given a number of learning experiences. You may pick and choose what you would like to do or you may create learning centers and allow the persons to move among them freely. For a model of setting up learning centers, see the session on God's Gift of Friendship on page 64.

View display

You will need: a variety of items from different countries (i.e., clothing, fabric, instruments, pottery, and other art work)

▶ Set up a display of items from various countries. Remind the learners that the people at Pentecost came from many countries outside of Palestine. Some of them traveled a long distance under difficult circumstances to be at this special celebration. The city became a worldwide marketplace of items brought by these people, hoping to find buyers.

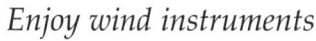

Enjoy wind instruments

You will need: recorders, kazoos, clarinets, flutes, and other wind instruments

▶ Contact families ahead of time and find out if any members of their families play one or more wind instruments. Invite them to bring the instrument to class.

▶ Use the instruments to play a simple tune. "Spirit of the Living God" might be a good tune to try.

▶ Talk about how wind or breath is a symbol of the Holy Spirit.

> Talk about how wind or breath is a symbol of the Holy Spirit.

Make posters

You will need: construction paper and markers

Make miniposters that say such things as:

• PENTECOST IS POWER
• PENTECOST PEOPLE ARE SPIRITED WITH HOLINESS
• WHEN THE SPIRIT CAME DOWN, OUR SPIRIT WENT UP
• THE SPIRIT OF PENTECOST: LET US SHARE CHRIST IN ALL LANGUAGES

Make puzzle of your church

You will need: an enlarged picture of your church, mounted on card stock, and cut into puzzle pieces.

▶ Set up a table for persons to put the puzzle together, or set aside a place on the floor. As you work, talk about the different opportunities for ministry to others and for learning about God that your church has to offer and how they would not be available if there had not first been a Pentecost.

Make flowing hoop-banners

You will need: wooden embroidery hoops, red and white ribbons, needle and thread

▶ Discuss ways that the Holy Spirit works in people's lives (i.e., guides, directs, inspires, leads, etc.).

▶ Give each person a red or white ribbon and ask them to write a verb on the ribbon that tells how the Holy Spirit works in people's lives. Wrap one end of the ribbon around the hoop and secure it with needle and thread.

▶ Use the flowing hoop-banners in your closing celebration, remembering how the Holy Spirit came as a rush of wind.

Cook different food

You will need: recipes from other countries and the ingredients for the various dishes

▶ Prior to class search for simple recipes from a variety of other countries and assemble the ingredients. Allow the learners to choose what they would like to cook. Enjoy the products of their work.

Translating on computer

You will need: computer and Internet connection

▶ Translate phrases using the Internet. Use www.Translation. Langenberg.Com, www.freetranslation.com, or a search engine to find another site by searching for "language translations."

▶ Remind learners that the people in the community at the first Pentecost spoke many different languages and the Holy Spirit enabled them to communicate and understand what was being said.

Use the flowing hoop-banners in your closing celebration, remembering how the Holy Spirit came as a rush of wind.

CELEBRATING THE THEME

You will need: hymnals

▶ Assign the following greeting (i.e., Peace be with you.) in different languages to various families in the class. As you begin your celebrating time, everyone will say their greeting at one time using their assigned language. [If you used the activity "Translating on the computer" use the translations that were found.]

English	Peace be with you.
French	Tranquillité être à vous.
Portuguese	Paz ser contigo.
Swedish	Freden vara med du.
Japanese	Kapayapaan maaari ka.

▶ Sing one of the following songs: "Come, Christians Join to Sing," "Let Us Break Bread Together," "They Will Know We Are Christians by Our Love," or "Surely the Presence of the Lord Is in This Place."

▶ Use the following litany and have them wave the hoop-banners each time they respond.

Voice 1:	We gather in this place, much as the early Christians did.
ALL:	**COME DOWN HOLY SPIRIT, IN WIND AND FIRE.**
Voice 2:	Let your love be around us.
Voice 3:	Let your strength be within us.
ALL:	**COME DOWN HOLY SPIRIT, IN WIND AND FIRE.**
Voice 1:	As with the wind, we feel your presence.
Voice 2:	Like a flame, God's love can grow in our hearts.
Voice 3:	We dedicate our lives to Thee.
ALL:	**COME DOWN HOLY SPIRIT, IN WIND AND FIRE.**[*]

* "Celebrate Pentecost," *Elementary B Church & Home Leaflets*, June 10, 1984, Nashville: Graded Press.

> "Come down Holy Spirit, in wind and fire."

Thanksgiving Becomes "Thanks-living"

Focus: *To explore the many things we are thankful for and ways we can express our thanks every day.*

Scripture: Psalm 111:1-6

INTRODUCTION TO THE THEME

Make miniposters

You will need: construction paper, markers or crayons

▶ As the learners enter, ask them to each make a miniposter showing something for which they are thankful. It may be something to eat, a person, an act that a person has done, and so on.

Illustrate hymn

You will need: large newsprint or poster board, markers or crayons

▶ Ask a youth or adult to print the words of the first two verses of "Come Ye Thankful People, Come." Ask others in the class to add illustrations around the verses.

EXPERIENCING THE THEME

Review miniposters

▶ Come together in a circle and ask each person to tell something about the poster he or she made. Encourage them to tell something about why they chose a specific item or object.

Create poster litany

▶ After all have shared, create a poster litany. To do this, each person will stand, hold up his or her miniposter, and state "I thank God for

---

(the subject of the miniposter)." After each person, the group will **say: "For this and other blessings, we give thanks."**

After everyone has participated, close with a prayer statement and **say: "Our God, we have thanked you for many things. There are many more gifts that you have given us. Help us to be aware of them every day. Amen."**

Tour your town

Make plans to tour your area of town and find things for which you are thankful. These might be physical things, teachers, community helpers, music, and so on. Share your findings through drawing, writing, recording an audio cassette about your experiences. You might use a video recorder or digital camera on the tour. If you have computer access, you may use it.

RESPONDING TO THE THEME

Make thank-you puppets

You will need: paper lunch bags, newspaper, markers, construction paper, scissors, glue, ribbons and lace or bits of fabric.

▶ Make paper bag puppets. As you work, talk about the many opportunities to thank God that we let slip by every day. Ask: **What would the world be like if God hadn't given us colors? Have you noticed the different textures of different tree trunks? What does freshly cut grass feel like to your bare feet?**

1. Roll up a small amount of newspaper and place it in the bottom of the bag.
2. Place a hand inside and then turn the bag upside down. Cut small holes on the sides for your thumb and little finger. These fingers will be the arms of the puppet.
3. Mark a line around the bag, just above the finger holes. This will be the neck.
4. Remove the stuffing and make happy facial features on the front of the bag. Draw the hair, or glue strips of curled paper to the bag for the hair.
5. Decorate the lower part of the bag as a dress or shirt. Add lace or pieces of fabric if desired.

6. Put the newspaper stuffing back into the bag, leaving room for the three middle fingers. Tie a ribbon or strip of cloth around the neck, or place a rubber band to secure the neck.

Respond with puppets

You will need: selection of items from home and out-of-doors. Place them in a large box. (See suggested items below.)

▶ Come together in a circle and ask each person to put his or her puppet on a hand. Place the items on a table in front of the group as you discuss them. **Say:**

In this box I have items that we see and use every day. You may take turns reaching into the box with your puppet and pulling out an item. Then talk for your puppet and tell us what your item is used for. After you have told us, we will all hold our puppets and put the "hands" of the puppets together while I say a sentence prayer of thanks.

The sentence prayers you give may be something like this:

Item	Prayer
Apple	Thank you, God, for the crisp taste of the apple.
Bright flower	Thank you, God, for giving us colors instead of making the world in black and white.
Picture of dog	Thank you, God for pets that we can enjoy.
Picture of night sky	Thank you, God, for the night to rest.
Picture of family	Thank you, God, for our families.
School supplies	Thank you, God for the chance to learn new things.
Toy car	Thank you, God, for making people with brains that know how to make cars so that we can ride long distances.
Box of raisins	Thank you, God, for those who process and package our food.
Toy truck	Thank you, God, for those who deliver our food from the farms to the stores.
Bandage	Thank you, God, for doctors and nurses who help when we are sick.

Bible	Thank you, God, for those who tell us about you in the Bible.
Baby clothing	Thank you, God, for your plan for us to grow into bigger boys and girls and adults.
Food seed package	Thank you, God, for seeds to grow food and for those who plant and grow our food.
Audiotape/CD of music	Thank you, God, for beautiful music.

CELEBRATING THE THEME

You will need: small "worship" table, cloth, candle, matches, items used in "Respond with puppets" above and illustrated hymn, Bible

▶ Place all of the items that you used in "Respond with puppets" on a cloth-covered small worship table. Light the candle and tell the learners that the light of the candle reminds us that God is here among us.

▶ Ask someone to read Psalm 111:1-6.

▶ Using the illustrated poster made at the beginning of the class, sing "Come Ye Faithful People, Come."

▶ Close asking everyone to "line" the following prayer after you. (You as leader will say a line and the participants will repeat it.) Say:

Our God, we come together to praise you today.
> You have given us many great things.
> Help us to remember you every day.
> Help us to be thankful of everything that surrounds us.
> Amen.

Part 3

SESSION SUGGESTIONS

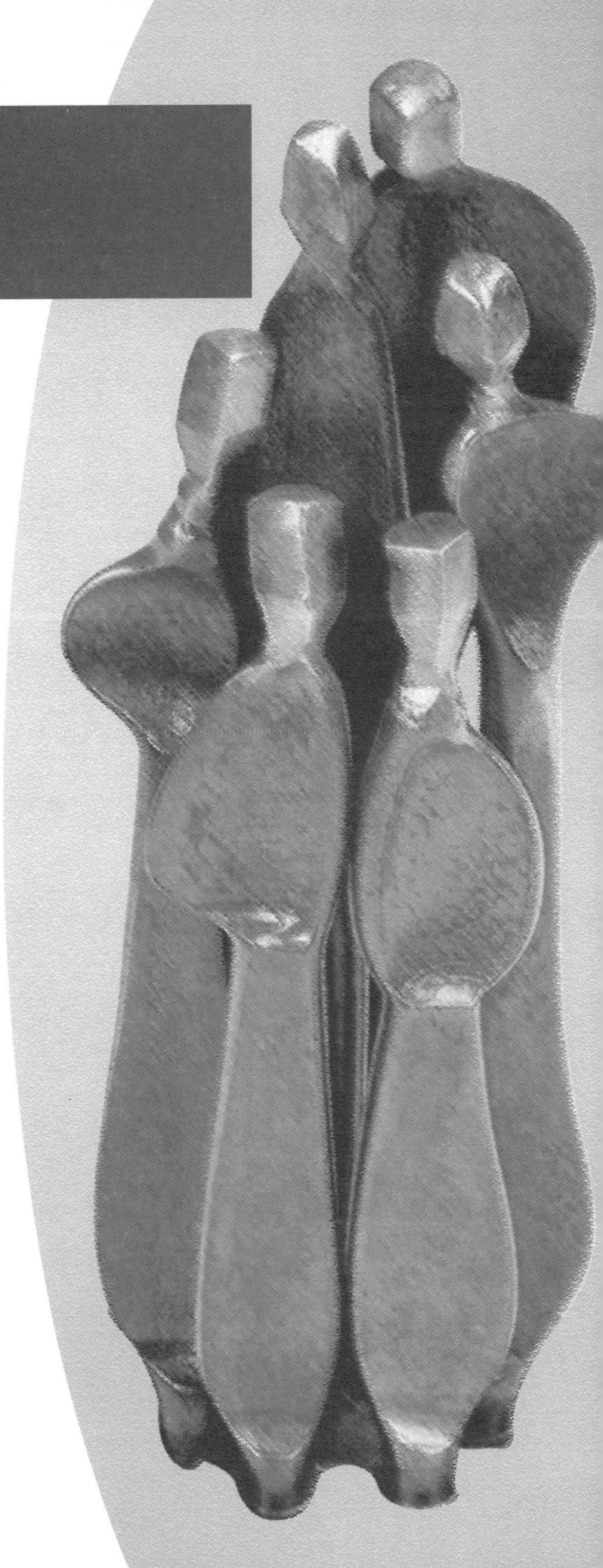

How to Use
This Section

A great number of possible activities for learning about the topics included in this section are available. Rather than providing specific lessons, I have instead listed a variety of suggestions from which you are free to pick and choose. You may choose to use the learning experiences presented here in one session or create a series of sessions on a particular topic.

In addition, you can select the way you want to set up a session(s) by using a regular Sunday school format or a learning center format. The session on "God's Gift of Friendship" on page 64 is specifically written to use activity or learning centers, where the family groups can move from center to center freely. Take note of this as a possible format for other sessions. Also remember to include all members of a family unit in one group when working in small groups.

I have suggested hymns or songs on these topics. You may use them during a gathering time at the beginning or close of each session if you select the learning center format. If you select a regular Sunday school format, use the hymns at any time it seems appropriate.

Finally, when using these session suggestions, if class members do not know one another, open the lesson with an activity that will help them get acquainted. Be sure to also include an activity of praise (ex.-a hymn) for the entire class at the close of the session.

Baptism: A Sacrament

Focus: *To help parents and children better understand the meaning of baptism.*

Scripture: Matthew 3:13-17

LEARNING AND WORSHIP OPPORTUNITIES

▶ Make name tags using a shell pattern. Explain that the shell is a symbol of baptism.

▶ Set up a worship center with white cloth, a pitcher of water, a bowl, small white towel, cross, candle. Pour water from the pitcher into the bowl, lifting the pitcher high so as to make a splashing noise when it falls. Ask individuals who would like, to come up and run their fingers through the water and put the water on their faces, remembering the meaning of baptism.

▶ Discuss the meaning of the word "sacrament" with the following information. **Say:**

> **The word sacrament means literally sacred moment, a time when humans come in contact with the divine. Most Protestant churches observe two sacraments, *baptism* and *communion,* which Jesus commanded us to observe. These events help us to taste, touch, feel, know, and experience the grace (or special love) of God. This grace is an unqualified, undeserved love. We receive grace without earning it. God's love says that even when at times we do not act in the way that God wants us to, God's love is there. Sometimes God loves with a happy heart, and sometimes God loves with a sad heart. But God always loves. We experience that love in the sacraments.**

▶ Research water in several books, or use a computer encyclopedia.

▶ Explore different types of shells. If you can get several examples, give a shell to each person. Talk about how the shell is a symbol we use to think of baptism.

▶ Read and discuss "Water Facts" from Handout #18.

▶ Search magazines for pictures of water in various forms and that is being used in different ways. Make a collage by gluing the pictures on a large sheet of paper. Divide them into these categories:

Water gives life   We cannot live without God.
Water cleanses us   God cleans us of wrongs.
Water refreshes us God refreshes us.

▶ List on chalkboard or large sheet of paper the different uses of water in the pictures from the above activity. Add any others. Explain that we use water as a symbol of baptism. It helps us remember that when we've done something wrong and ask for forgiveness, God forgives, like washing the wrong away.

▶ Ask for persons to share some times they have been very dirty. After each story of being sweaty and dirty, ask the person how it felt to get cleaned up. After everyone has shared, ask how these stories remind you of baptism.

▶ Read the story of Jesus' baptism from Matthew 3:13-17.

▶ Make bookmarks for Jesus' baptism. Put the appropriate scripture location on each bookmark.

▶ Using building blocks, make a baptismal font like one in your church.

▶ Find the place of Jesus' baptism on a map of Palestine.

▶ After reading the story of Jesus' baptism, act it out. Costumes are not necessary.

▶ Take a story walk. Before class write the following words on large footprints that have been cut from construction paper. Tape these in order on the floor, and the learners will walk on the footprints and read the story as they walk.

- John the Baptist wore strange clothes and ate insects and honey!
- John told people that God wanted them to be better persons.
- John baptized those who were sorry for what they had done wrong.

Water

gives life.

Water

cleanses us.

Water

refreshes us.

- One day Jesus came to the river.
- He asked John to baptize him.
- John said, "No, I should be baptized by you instead!"
- Jesus said, "God wants you to baptize me."
- And so John baptized Jesus.
- God's spirit came to Jesus like a dove.
- After his baptism, Jesus went to a place where he could be alone.
- There he talked to God about what he should do. (Matthew 3–17)

▶ Talk about the three ways of baptizing (*sprinkling, pouring,* and *immersion*). With any of these methods we become a part of God's family. Explain to the children that if they were baptized as an infant their parents made certain promises for them, and when they are older they will decide whether to accept the promises for themselves. If they were not baptized as infants, they can make the choice to be baptized themselves.

▶ Review the baptismal service, explaining any words that are not understood.

▶ Visit the baptismal font in the sanctuary. Use a pitcher to pour water in the font at a height so that it makes a sound. Give everyone an opportunity to feel the water.

▶ View a video of a baptism. Discuss how it is similar or different from a baptism they have seen.

▶ Prior to the session, ask learners to bring reminders of their baptism or of the baptism of someone else. During the session, ask families to share the reminders of baptism that they might have brought. There are likely to be fancy dresses or similar items. Assure everyone that the way the person is dressed does not make a difference in the baptism.

▶ Discuss other ways that individuals can welcome someone into God's family when they are baptized. (for example, —talking with, calling by name, reading or telling a Bible story, etc.)

▶ Make a gift that can be given at a future baptism. This might be a crib sheet (or pillow case for an older child) with pictures of water drawn on it and a message from each person. Be sure to use permanent markers or fabric crayons, and remember to wash the gift before presenting it.

▶ Make a poster, welcoming a person who will be baptized soon into the Family of God.

▶ Light candles and remember that the light symbolizes Christ.

▶ Sing "I Am the Church! You Are the Church!" As you sing, take a bowl of water and walk among the learners, allowing each person to lift a handful of water and let it run back into the bowl.

▶ Pray a similar prayer to this one. **Say: Our God, we thank you that each of us is a part of your church. We remember that you give us life and forgive our wrongs. Amen.**

Create a *cinquain* (sin cane) poem together. Use it in your closing worship. To do this, ask persons to suggest words or phrases for each line listed below. Record the suggestions.

Say: Line 1: **Baptism**
Line 2: **Two words about baptism**
Line 3: **Three action words about baptism**
Line 4: **Four "feeling" words telling of baptism (these may end in "-ing").**
Line 5: **One word that means the same as baptism or "Amen"**
Place the words in this order.

————

———— ————

———— ———— ————

———— ———— ———— ————

————

▶ Sing one of these songs or a similar tune: "Take My Life and Let It Be," "Child of Blessing, Child of Promise," "A Charge to Keep I Have," "Here I Am, Lord," "Let There Be Peace on Earth, and Let It Begin with Me."

The Bible: What About It?

[**NOTE:** Whether you choose to make this one session or a series of 4 to 6 sessions will depend on your learners, how well they know the Bible, and how in-depth you want to make the study.]

Focus: *To explore our Bible and become familiar with its contents and where it came from.*

Scripture: 2 Timothy 3:16-17

LEARNING AND WORSHIP OPPORTUNITIES

▶ *Bring a Bible.* Ask learners to bring their Bibles prior to starting the session. Also, assure them that Bibles will be available if they do not have one.

▶ *What is scripture for?* Read 2 Timothy 3:16-17. Discuss the purpose of our scriptures. Be sure to go beyond verse 16 and emphasize verse 17.

▶ *Explore translations:* Have a variety of translations and styles of Bibles on hand, some with study helps, some with concordances, some with maps, and some gift Bibles. If your number is small, you may do this all together, but if you have a larger group, set up several "stations" with 3-4 different Bibles at each station. Divide the learners into groups and have them rotate among the stations, taking notes about the differences they discover in each Bible. After they have visited all stations, ask them to share their findings about how the Bibles are different.

▶ *Describe books:* Ask the learners to describe various books that they have read. Talk about different types of books: fiction, nonfiction, biographies, text books, how-to books, travel books, poetry, collections of stories, and so on. Tell them that the Bible is not like any of these books, and yet a little like all of them. Perhaps the best way to explain the Bible is to recognize that it is a book about how people came to understand God better. It is like a library put together in one book. Give each person a copy of Handout #11 and look at the number of books in each category.

Assign various books of the Bible for them to look up by using the Table of Contents. Explain that it is helpful to memorize the books of the Bible in order, but that it is not necessary. Provide bookmarks that can be placed into the Table of Contents and encourage them to use them.

▶ *Remember favorite Bibles.* Ask the participants to talk about Bibles that they have or have had in the past, how they got them, how they are different from other Bibles, and why they like them. If there is an interesting story about one of the Bibles, ask the person to share it.

▶ *Learn about Bible references.* Prior to the session, copy Handout #12 so that each person has a copy. Ask each person to open the Bible to the Table of Contents. Assign them to work in groups of three, each paired with another group, and suggest that parents help their children with this assignment. Ask the groups to follow the instructions on Handout #12. After the groups have had time to work, assign these scriptures for them to look up accordingly:

1) Look up the following books: *Old Testament* books:
   • A book of law: Exodus
   • A book of history: 2 Kings
   • A book of wisdom: Ecclesiastes
   • A book of prophets: Amos

In the *New Testament* look up these books:
   • A gospel: Luke
   • A book of history: Acts
   • A book of letters: Colossians

2) Look up the book of Isaiah in the Old Testament and see how many chapters it has in it.
   Then, look up the book of Philemon in the New Testament and see how many chapters it has.

3) Look up the following scripture verses:
   • Proverbs 3:5-6
   • Matthew 19:14
   • Luke 12:25
   • 1 Corinthians 13:13

4) Look up the following verses:
- Psalm 86:11*a*
  - Ecclesiastes 7:8*b*
    - Hebrews 12:1*a*
    - James 1:19*b*

▶ *Find hidden names of books in Bible.* Using Handout #15, have family groups work together to find the hidden names of the books in the Bible. Printed below are the answers to handout. Note that the name can use letters from two words.

Here are some re<u>mark</u>s about the Bible. <u>Numbers</u> of the readers will have the <u>revelation</u> of the <u>truth</u> about the Bible. The stories were first told around campfires and in the homes. Sometimes they used walls of caves or clay tablets to write on. Then they were written on the skins of animals and later on a fiber made from plants. These skins and pounded fiber were rolled into scrolls for easy carrying. Y<u>es, there</u> were real books later, but then they had to be copied by hand. This was usually done by a monk. <u>He brews</u> over the manuscript, loo<u>king s</u>o hard at his work. Mistakes could easily happen. You can <u>judge s</u>o for yourself. The monks who copied the scriptures would probably adm<u>it it u</u>sually resulted in loud <u>lamentations</u> when they worked long hours.

Sometimes the <u>job</u> of translating the Bible puts the translators in a <u>jam, es</u>pecially when the word in one language does not have an exact meaning in another. But some people find it <u>a most</u> fascinating puzzle. This work is a real lu<u>lu, keeping</u> the translators looking so hard for <u>facts.</u>

▶ *Make clay tablets.* Mix one cup of salt, ½ cup of cornstarch, ½ cup of boiling water in a cooking pan. Place the pan over low heat. Stir the mixture constantly. The clay will become stiff. When the clay has cooled, knead it until it is smooth. The clay will be white. Before the clay hardens, form your tablet and use a stick to print your favorite Bible verse.[1]

1. From *Discovering How the Bible Came to Be* by Becky Atkinson (Vacation Bible School, Grades 5-6 Student Book), Nashville: Graded Press © 1983, page 24. Used by permission.

• *Make ink.* Use ripe berries to make colored ink. Use ½ cup of any type of berry that is the color you want. Pour the berries into a strainer over a bowl. Mash them with the smooth back of a wooden spoon until all the juice is in the bowl. Throw away what is left in the strainer. Add ½ teaspoon of vinegar to keep the ink from fading. Add ½ teaspoon of salt to keep the ink from getting moldy. Stir until well mixed. If the ink is too thick, add a few drops of water. Pour the berry ink into a small jar with a lid that closes tightly. Make only a small amount of ink at a time. Keep the lid on when not using the ink. (After a while your ink may turn to jelly. It should not be eaten.)[2]

Try writing verses with a feather or sharp stick dipped in ink, much like the Bible was written before printed books.

• *Hebrew Alphabet.* Using the Hebrew Alphabet Code in Handout #13, have the learners work in pairs or threes to break the code and find the words that the prophet Hosea spoke for God.

• *Translations.* Tell the class that the Bible was not originally written in English. The Old Testament was written in Hebrew and the New Testament was written in Greek. Copy Handout #14 for the learners to read and work with.

• *Learn a method of finding books in Bible.* Be sure that each person has a Bible. Young children will need help from adults. Use Handout #16 to teach an easy way to find the books of the Bible. Handout #11 will help with this activity also.

• *Make devotional booklet.* Ask each family to write a devotion on a favorite Bible story or passage. The form on Handout #17 will help them format the devotion. Make copies of the devotions they write and give the copies to members of the church.

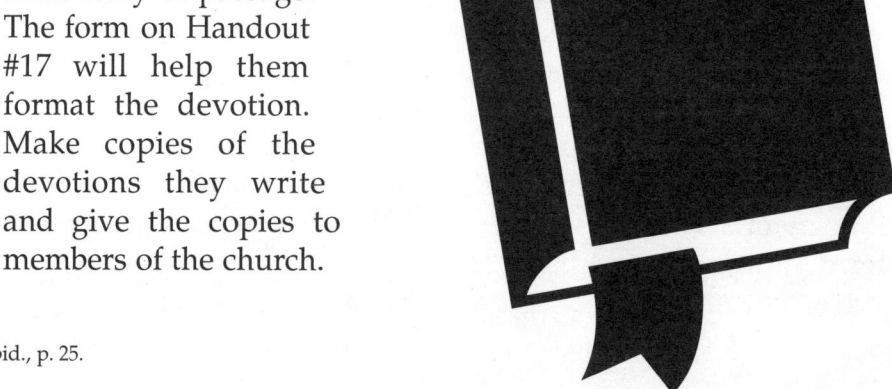

2. Ibid., p. 25.

▶ *Tell story in echo pantomime.* Ask the group what an echo is, and then ask what a pantomime is. Tell them that in the echo pantomime you will give a sentence with actions, and then they will all repeat the sentence with actions. Try the one below, and then the class may want to create one themselves, using a different Bible story.

SOLOMON BUILDS A TEMPLE
(Echo pantomime based on 1 Kings 5 and 6)

Words	Actions
Long ago people lived in tents.	Shape tent with hands over head.
They worshiped God in tents too.	Step to side, shape another tent.
God planned for King Solomon to build a temple.	Make crown for king.
There were many workers for God.	Point to many people.
Some cut the cedar trees.	Turn right and cut with ax.
Some cut the cypress trees.	Turn left and cut with ax.
Some dug stones from hills.	Dig with shovel.
Some hammered the wood.	Hammer.
Some put stones together.	Pile stones together.
Finally the Temple was finished.	Spread out arms and smile.
Everyone sang and shouted with joy!	Cup hands around mouth.
And the celebration to God began.	March in circle, clapping or playing on instrument.[3]

3. *New Ways to Tell the Old, Old Story* by Delia Halverson (Nashville: Abingdon Press, 1992), p. 36. Used by permission.

▶ *Recreate oral tradition.* Create an imaginary campfire using pieces of wood, crumpled yellow and red cellophane paper, and a flashlight under the paper. Sit around the campfire as you tell Bible stories. Remind the learners that this is how our Bible first began.

▶ *Make stained glass window.* You will need typing weight paper, black construction paper, pencils, crayons, scissors, black permanent marker, cooking oil, and cotton swabs.

1. You can pre-cut frames the shape of windows from the black construction paper, cutting out the space where the picture will show through.
2. Have a conversation about how stained glass windows were used when very few people could read. The windows told the Bible stories when people didn't have Bibles to read the stories.
3. Have each person decide on a Bible story they want to illustrate.
4. Place the pre-cut construction paper frame over the white paper and trace the outline of the opening where the picture will show through. (After the picture is finished, the "opening" area will be treated with oil, but the area outside the "opening" will be left white and not treated with oil.)
5. Inside the area that was outlined, learners will draw the picture in simple lines, tracing over the lines with permanent marker. This represents the "leaded" part of the stained glass.
6. Using crayons, color all parts inside the opening area, including the background.
7. Protect the working surface with papers, and using cotton swabs dipped in cooking oil, coat the *back* side of the drawing only, being careful not to use the oil outside the colored area. Wipe away any excess oil with paper towels.
8. Glue the frame around the picture.

▶ *Find Bible helps.* The Bible helps us to know God better. Look up one or more of these scriptures and paraphrase the verses. They may also be illustrated if learners would like.

When you feel alone and afraid	Hebrews 13:5b-7
When you want to blame other people for your mistake	1 John 1:8-9
When you don't want to do what you should	Romans 7:14-25
When you are about to give up trying	Philippians 3:13-14
When you feel the most important thing is to be first	Matthew 20:20-28

When you can't make peace with someone	Romans 12:14-21
When you can't seem to overcome worry	Matthew 6:25-34
When someone you love dies	Romans 8:35-39[4]

- *Enjoy scavenger hunt.* Go on a scavenger hunt in the Bible, using a concordance. Give each group several scripture passages. Using a concordance and the Bible, the group will work together to find the correct passage and list it. Here are some suggestions for verses and their references. Only give the groups the words from the verses.

- But the angel said to them, "Do not be afraid. . . ."   Luke 1:13*a*

- What God has made clean, you must not call profane." Acts 10:15*b*

- Do you not know that you are God's temple and that God's Spirit dwells in you?   1 Corinthians 3:16

- I am the first and I am the last; besides me there is no god. Isaiah 44:6*b*

- Commit your work to the LORD, and your plans will be established. Proverbs 16:3

- I will praise the name of God with a song. . . . Psalm 69:30*a*

- "Where were you when I laid the foundation of the earth?"   J o b 38:4*a*

- Your people shall be my people, and your God my God. Ruth 1:16*c*

- But as for me and my household, we will serve the LORD. Joshua 24:15*c*

▶ *Sing hymns about the Bible and hymns that come from scripture.* Look in the scripture index of your hymnal for hymns for specific scripture. Other hymns might include:
"I Love to Tell the Story"
"Tell Me the Stories of Jesus"
"Go, Tell It on the Mountain"

4. *How Do Our Children Grow?* by Delia Halverson, St. Louis: Chalice Press, 1999, page 65 (revised edition).

Communion: A Sacrament

Focus: *To provide information about the basis of our sacrament of communion and to help parents and children make it a meaningful part of their Christian experience.*

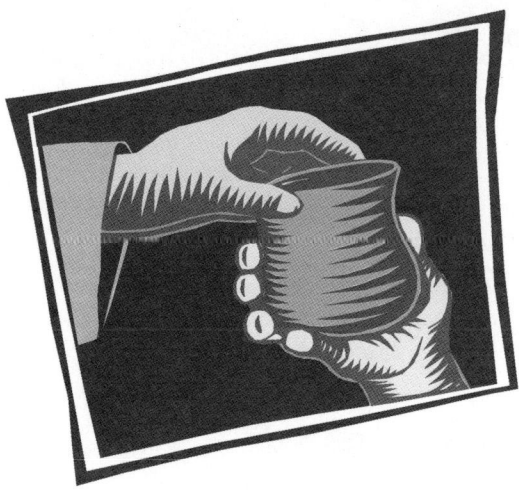

Scriptures: Luke 13:20-21; Luke 22:7-20; John 8:1-11

LEARNING CENTER OPPORTUNITIES

Place the instructions below at each center. The materials needed for each center are listed in parentheses.

▶ *Make name tags*—Draw your favorite food on a name tag. Find someone you don't know and introduce yourself, telling them about your favorite food. (*Materials: half-sheets of construction paper, hole punch, yarn to hang tag around neck*)

▶ *Learn about communion*—Read the following information about communion in your group. Recall communion services that you have attended that have been different in some way.

COMMUNION

▶ has its roots in the Passover which celebrates the time that God helped the Israelites to be free.

▶ is a way of remembering Jesus, particularly when he had the Passover meal with the disciples.

▶ is acting out Jesus' last supper, using the bread as a symbol of Jesus' body that was broken for us on the cross, and the juice or wine as a symbol of Jesus' blood that he shed for us.

▶ is a time to remember when we have done wrong and ask God to forgive us.

▶ is a way to bring Jesus closer to us and give us new strength to help others.

▶ is a time to celebrate with other Christians.

▶ is a time of great thanksgiving.

► *Make bread cloth*—Use crayons to put symbols on your cloth. A fabric that is part cotton and part polyester works best. When you get home, place the cloth face down on clean paper and iron it on the wrong side. You may also fray or hem the edges. Use your cloth for special meals with your family. *(Materials: Paper to cover table, 18-inch squares of white fabric, crayons, sample cloth)*

► *Make grape juice*—Put a few grapes into a juicer and make juice for the session. If a juicer is not available, substitute a blender or food processor, or press the juice using a wooden spoon and a strainer. The latter method yields very little juice. *(Materials: grapes and juicer, food processor, or strainer and wooden spoon, cups)*

► *Enjoy wheat*—Look at the pictures of wheat in the field and the stalks of wheat. Let some of the wheat grain run through your fingers. Think about other grains that are used to make bread. Try crushing some wheat and tasting it. Compare the whole grains of wheat with the prepared flour. Read about making bread. *(Materials: pictures, wheat stalks/grains of wheat, stones or mortar and pestle for crushing wheat, processed flour, and books about making bread)*

► *Knead bread*—Experiment with kneading bread. Read Luke 13:20-21 and talk about how our love is like leaven or yeast, growing when we use it. *(Materials: Bible, fresh dough or frozen bread dough that has thawed, cleaned table or bread board, flour to keep dough from sticking, handwashing capability)*

► *Look at communion preparation*—Look at the items that we use for communion. Some churches use a large cup or chalice and dip bread into the juice. Other churches use small individual cups. Try using the communion cup filler to fill a cup with juice. You may drink the juice that you pour. *(Materials: juice, chalice, small cups, communion cup filler, bowl or pan to catch drips when pouring, paper towels)*

► *Make a forgiveness stone*—Read the story in John 8:1-11. Make a forgiveness stone by printing "First" on the side of a stone. Take this home to help you remember that we are asked to *first* confess our sins to God when we take communion. *(Materials: Bible, stones, permanent marker)*

► *Add to graffiti wall*—Draw pictures and symbols or write words to explain times that we need forgiveness. *(Materials: Large sheet of paper mounted on wall, crayons)*

◗ *Talk about favorite meals*—Look at the table setting and have a conversation about special meals that you have had with your family, or friends. *(Materials: placemat, plate, glass, flatware, napkin)*

◗ *Read scripture*—Read Luke 22:7-20 and ask the following questions:
- **How do you suppose the disciples felt when they were asked to prepare the place for the dinner?**
- **They did not have restaurants for special celebrations then. Where would you go for a special dinner if we didn't have restaurants?**
- **What would you ask one of the disciples about this meal if you could talk to him today?**

◗ *Make bookmarks*—Make bookmarks for the story of the Last Supper. Put the scripture passage on the bookmark and decorate it with symbols from communion. *(Materials: construction paper, scissors, markers or crayons)*

◗ *Locate places on map*—Look on a map and locate Egypt, where the first Passover happened. Trace the trip that the Hebrews took to go to Palestine. Locate Jerusalem, where Jesus had the Last Supper with his disciples. *(Materials: maps)*

◗ *Enjoy building blocks*—Using blocks and other items, build a Bible time house where Jesus and his friends had supper. *(Materials: blocks, etc.)*

Worship opportunity

◗ Light the candle at the worship center.
◗ Reread the verse that commands us to repeat the meal in remembrance of Jesus (Luke 22:19).
◗ Have a brief communion service.

[NOTE: If clergy is not available, have a "Love Feast" using bread and juice. For the Love Feast, use the table grace "Be Present at Our Table, Lord" and read a psalm or Matthew 22:34-40. Remember how Jesus ate the last meal with disciples he loved.]

Easter: Our Celebration

Focus: *To celebrate the renewal of life and the fact that God did not let Jesus stay dead.*

Scriptures: Matthew 28:1-10; Mark 16:1-8; Luke 24:1-12; John 20:1-18; Psalm 118:1-2, 14-24

LEARNING AND WORSHIP OPPORTUNITIES

Wax onions

Focus: *To recognize something that comes to life from something that appears dead.*

You will need: several small sprouting onions, empty vegetable cans, wax (paraffin or old candles), pieces of crayons, an old knife with a wooden handle (or a crayon melter), an electric frying pan

Directions:
1. Peel dry skin from the onions.
2. Place the wax in the vegetable cans. Use enough to cover the onions once it has melted, but be sure that you do not put so much in that it will spill over the top of the can when the onions are added.
3. Add crayon pieces of various colors to the wax in the cans. (Note: Food coloring will not work because it will not mix with wax.)
4. Place the cans with the wax in an electric fry pan. Fill the fry pan with water to about $1/4$ the height of the cans.
5. Bring the water to a simmer. If the water begins to boil dry, add more water. **Caution:** If the heated cans are not in water, they can become hot enough to catch on fire!
6. Stir occasionally with a stick.
7. Dip each onion in the melted wax. Hold it above the can for a few seconds to allow the wax to harden. Repeat the process until the onion is completely covered with wax and is the color you want. Note: If you leave the onion in the hot wax too long, the previous layers will melt.

8. Place the onions on paper towels until the wax is hardened.
9. Decorate the onions. Heat the blade of a wooden-handled knife. Touch the hot knife to crayons while holding them over one of the waxed onions. The crayon will melt and drip on the onion. (Another option is to use a "crayon melter" and drip the heated wax over the onions.)
10. Put the onions in a basket with Easter grass and enjoy them. **Note:** Keep the waxed onions away from heat, and the sprouts will continue to grow for some time. When they begin to wilt, use the spouts in a salad. Break the wax from around the bulb and plant it outdoors. It will grow another bulb.

Draw a sunshine picture

Focus: *To appreciate the sunshine that shines through darkness, as Christ's love for us came with his death.*

You will need: bright yellow (glossy) shelf paper, black crayons, blunt scissors or nonsharp table knives.

▶ Have the learners make "Sunshine pictures" by putting a coat of black wax crayon over the whole area of the bright yellow (glossy) shelf paper. Then they will create a picture of the sun shining through darkness by scraping off parts of the black crayon.

▶ After the pictures are made, share them with the class and talk about how Jesus' disciples were very sad, like living in a dark world, and how Easter morning brought sunshine to their lives.

Color eggs

Focus: *To appreciate new life that Christ gives us.*

You will need: hard boiled eggs (enough eggs to eat), Easter egg dye and containers for dipping eggs, plastic for work surface

▶ Set up equipment for coloring eggs. Be sure that the work surface is well protected.

▶ After dyeing the eggs, enjoy eating them and discuss the background and symbolism of dyeing the egg.

EASTER EGGS

The first book to mention Easter eggs was written over five hundred years ago; however, a tribe in North Africa traditionally colored eggs long before that. Some European countries make intricate designs on their eggs which take many hours. They use designs of flowers, wheat, fish, and other religious symbols. The eggs are then taken to church and blessed before they are given as tokens of love to friends.

For younger children: From the egg comes the chicken in springtime. All things are made new in spring. Jesus died but came to new life at Easter.

For older children, youth, and adults add: Christ is one way we understand God. Like there are three parts to an egg (example—shell, yolk, egg white), there are three ways that we understand God: *God our creator and sustainer, Jesus "God with skin on,"* and *the Holy Spirit, or God within us.* We sometimes call this the Trinity.

View newness in nature

Focus: *To become aware of the rebirth of nature that happens at Easter time.*

▶ Take a trip outside and ask the learners to look for signs of new birth, of things coming back to life after they seem to have been dead over the winter months. [Even if you live in the warmer climates, there are subtle signs of rebirth. For example, the leaves may not stay off the trees all winter, but new leaves grow and replace dead ones. Also, there are always new seeds sprouting.]

Make butterflies

Focus: *To recognize something that comes to life from something that appears dead.*

You will need: paper, pencils, scissors, crayons or markers (Note: If markers are used, use a card-stock weight paper to make the butterfly so that the markers don't bleed through.)

▶ Use the pattern on the next page to make caterpillars that become butterflies. Place the pattern on a fold in the paper and trace and cut the other edges. When the design is folded it will look like a caterpillar, but when unfolded it becomes a butterfly. Draw the mouth and eye on the outside and color the inside butterfly colors.

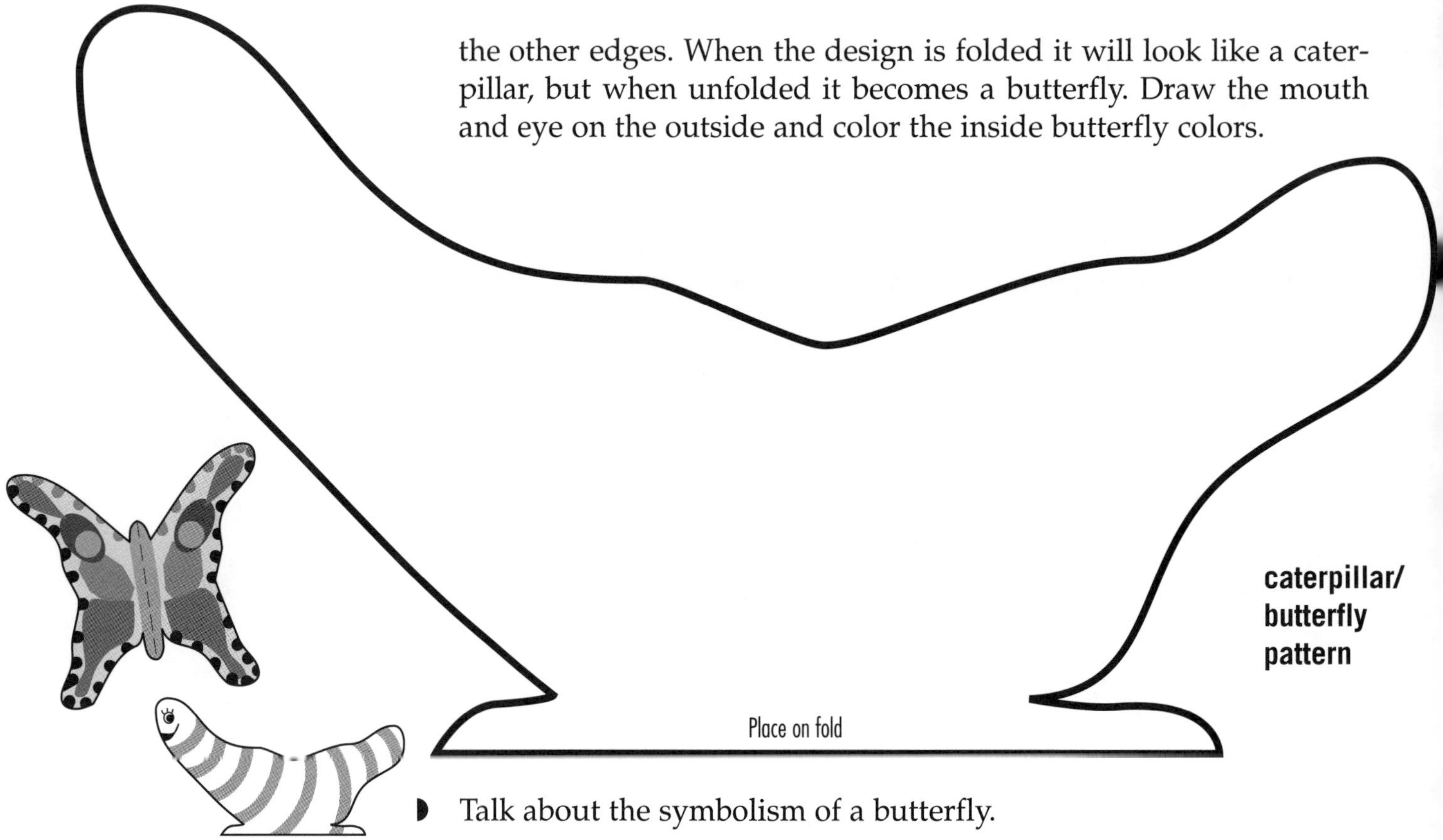

**caterpillar/
butterfly
pattern**

Place on fold

▶ Talk about the symbolism of a butterfly.

1. The caterpillar seems to die before changing into a lovely, graceful creature. We believe that our lives do not end in death but we have a future in God after death.

2. The life cycle of a butterfly might be compared to the three stages of a Christian life:

> *Caterpillar*—**life on earth**
> *chrysalis*—**our being in the grave**
> *butterfly*—**transformation to eternal life**

Make Easter lilies

Focus: *To recognize something that comes to life from something that appears dead.*

You will need: a bulb of a flower or an onion, white typing paper, green and yellow construction paper, pencils, scissors, stapler.

▶ Pass the dry bulb around the group, giving everyone a chance to examine it.

▶ Ask for ideas of what might happen to the bulb. (If it is an onion, it will also have a bloom.)

▶ To make a lily, trace a hand and 2-3 inches of the arm on the paper. Cut it out, including the 2-3 inches of the arm beyond the hand. Using a pencil, curl all of the paper fingers down. Beginning with the thumb side, roll the hand, leaving the fingers (which are curled out) loose at the top. Add a few strips of yellow paper inside the palm and then staple it all onto a long green paper stem.

Eat special food

Focus: *To recognize the symbolism of certain foods.*

Enjoy some of the traditional foods for Easter. Talk about why we eat these foods. The symbolism of some of these foods is listed below:

▶ Eggs remind us of spring and the newness of life. Christ's resurrection brought new life even after death.

▶ Easter breads: *paska* from the Ukraine; *hot cross buns* from England that remind us of the cross where Jesus died before his resurrection; the *festival loaf* from Greece; and *babka* from Poland. Some Easter breads bake a whole egg in the bread. The yeast in the bread reminds us that when we keep Christ in our lives our love grows and expands to others.

▶ Cookies in the shape of a lamb remind us that Christ was called the Lamb of God. In ancient times believers made offerings to God by burning a lamb on their altars. We believe that Jesus' death was the ultimate offering to God. Lambs are born in the spring and remind us of new life.

View collection of crosses

Focus: *To appreciate why we use an empty cross.*

You will need: a collection of crosses of all types (include at least one with the crucifix on it), picture of the cross in your sanctuary, Handout #7.

▶ Display a variety of crosses. Ask the learners to look at the different crosses. Pass those that can be handled around the group.

▶ Ask learners which cross they like best and why.

▶ Look at the picture of the cross in your sanctuary. [If there is time, make a trip to the sanctuary and anywhere else in the church buildings where you have crosses.]

▶ **Ask: Why do we use an empty cross?** *(Because we know that God didn't let Jesus remain dead, and we celebrate a risen Christ)*

▶ Discuss the various crosses on Handout #7.

▶ Sing "Christ the Lord Is Risen Today" or "He Lives" or another appropriate Easter song.

Research butterflies on Internet

Focus: *To appreciate the symbolism of the butterfly.*

You will need: a computer with Internet access.

▶ Visit several sites to find out more about butterflies. Choose an encyclopedia site or www.butterflywebsite.com

    ▶ Enjoy an interactive site with butterflies at http://home.columbus.rr.com/cheztonner/butterflies.html

        ▶ Talk about the symbolism of the butterfly that appears under the "Make butterflies" activity above.

      Release butterflies

      Focus: *to appreciate the symbolism of the butterfly.*

      You will need: butterflies that have emerged from their chrysalis. These can be ordered from 1-800-LIVE-BUG or the web sites: *www.insectlore.com* or *www.butterflywebsite.com*

      ▶ Sing an Easter hymn.

      ▶ Talk about the symbolism of the butterfly that appears under the "Make butterflies" activity above.

      ▶ Give a prayer of dedication and thanks for the butterflies, asking God to lift our hearts as the butterflies are lifted into the air on their lovely wings.

      ▶ Release the butterflies.

Reflect on Sundays and Easter

Focus: *To connect Sundays with Easter.*

You will need: Bible

▶ Ask different people to read the following verses: Genesis 2:2-3; Exodus 20:8-11; Exodus 31:15-16; Deuteronomy 5:12-15; Mark 2:23-27; Luke 4:16.

▶ Ask:
 • **What did the Bible say about the Sabbath?**

- **When is the Sabbath?**
- **When does the Jewish religion celebrate the Sabbath?**
- **Why do we celebrate the Sabbath on Sunday?** *(because Jesus was raised from the dead on Sunday)*

Read and discuss a psalm

Focus: *To celebrate the joy and victory of Easter*

You will need: Bible

▶ Ask someone to read Psalm 118:1-2, 14-24.

▶ **Ask:**
- **What sort of feelings were expressed in the Psalm?** *(joy and victory)*
- **How do those feelings relate to Easter?**

▶ Reread verse 24. This verse literally reads, "This is the day on which the Lord has acted mightily."
Easter celebrates the greatest victory we know. With Easter we believe that God is greater than everything, even death. God can conquer all.

Give balloon messages

Focus: *To celebrate the greatest gift.*

You will need: balloons, strips of paper, pencils

▶ Give class members strips of paper and pencils and ask them to write an Easter message for someone else. The message might be something like: "He is risen!" "Rejoice in the Lord." "He lives today too!"

▶ Each message will be placed inside a balloon and then the balloon will be blown up and the end secured. The balloons may be inflated ahead of time and the messages written on cards and tied to the outside of the balloons. Use the balloons in your closing time together, and then they may be given to friends or taken to the church service and given to church members.
(**NOTE:** If you use helium balloons, make certain that they are not released into the air where they may be harmful to birds and other animals.)

Pray together

Focus: *To offer a prayer of praise and thanksgiving.*

▶ Use the prayer below or use one of your own. This may be lined with the learners repeating the prayer after you. **Say:**

**O God, your Son said he is the resurrection and the life.
Make me aware of his presence today.
May we find joy, even when we are sad.
May we share that joy with others.
Amen.**

Sing Easter songs

Focus: *To raise our voices in praise.*

You will need: hymnals or words printed on chalkboard or newsprint

▶ Select one or more of the hymns below or look for additional ones in the index of your hymnal.

**"Christ the Lord Is Risen Today"
"Come, Christians, Join to Sing"
"Crown Him with Many Crowns"
"Cristo Vive (Christ Is Risen)"
"Easter People, Raise Your Voices"
"Fairest Lord Jesus"
"He Lives"**

**"Joyful, Joyful We Adore Thee"
"Let All the World in Every Corner Sing"
"Morning Has Broken"
"This Is the Day"
"Up from the Grave He Arose"
"When Morning Gilds the Skies"**

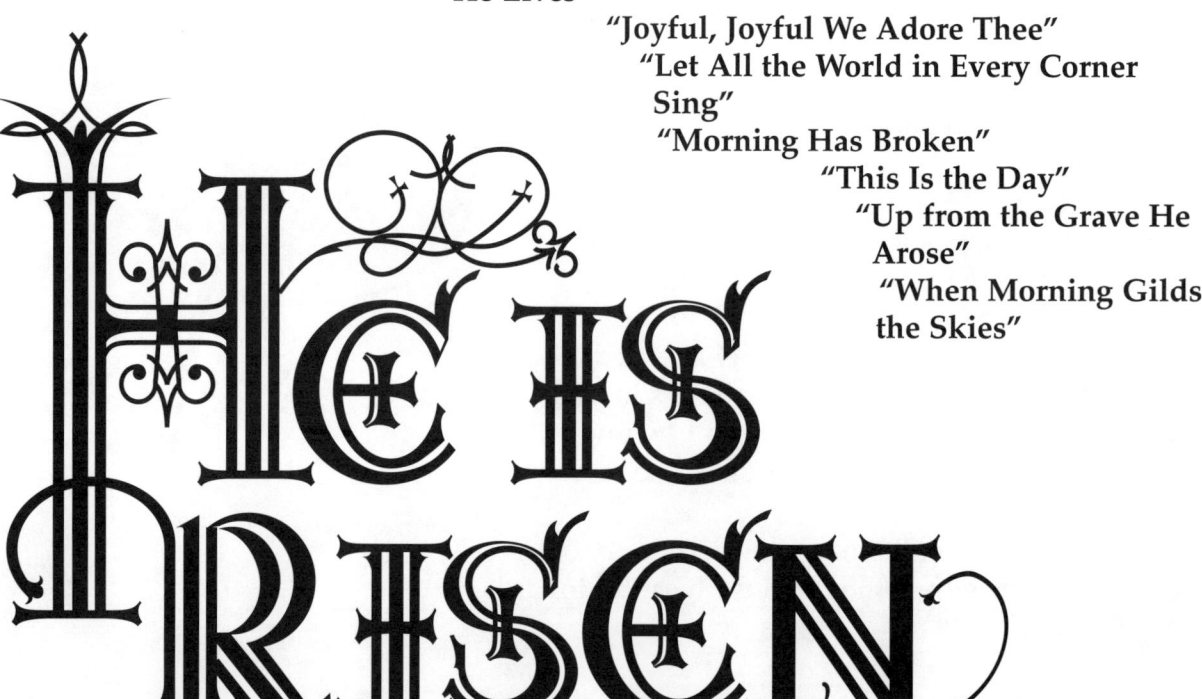

Nature: A Way to Learn of God

Focus: *To explore many of the ways that God is seen as dependable in our world.*

Scripture: Genesis 8:22

LEARNING AND WORSHIP OPPORTUNITIES

▶ *Make seasons picture.* Using light construction paper, each person will divide a page into four equal parts. Next, draw a picture of one of the four seasons of the year in each part of the page. If you live in an area that does not have a drastic change of seasons, suggest that learners think of subtle changes, such as the season that certain trees bloom, or the season when school is out, and so on. After the pictures are completed, ask each person to share what he or she has drawn. Read Genesis 8:22.

▶ *Make seasons collage.* Use four large sheets of paper, one for each season. Invite the class members to draw or find pictures in magazines to indicate different things that happen in each of the four seasons. Glue the pictures onto the appropriate pieces of paper. If you live in a climate that does not have drastic change in seasons, draw or find pictures of trees and flowers in bloom or specific activities your community participates in during the seasons. When the collage is complete discuss the collage with the entire class and read Genesis 8:22.

▶ *Illustrate God's creation as the story is told.* Using a long roll of paper divided into the six sections listed below, ask family groups to illustrate specific sections while you tell the story. Play a recording of nature sounds as the groups work on the mural. After completion, post the mural in your room or in the hall for others to enjoy.
- **light/dark**
- **water and sky** (with nothing in the sky or water)
- **dry land with plants of all types** (If you have more than six

family groupings, this section might be larger than the others and several family groups assigned to work here.

- **sun, moon, and stars**
- **fish and birds**
- **men, women, and children**

❿ *Discover God's world through touch.* This is done in family units with everyone holding hands. Blindfold one person from each family unit with an adult in front of each line. The groups move to different places, stopping to ask the blindfolded person to explore the objects (for example, trees, rock, soft dirt, and grass) without using sight. Be certain they are holding hands as you move from place to place, and watch that you don't go over unexpected step-ups and downs without telling each person when to step. The blindfold may be changed to other family members from time to time.

❿ *Plant a tree or bush.* Using a prepared site, plant a tree together. As you work, talk about how God gave us this lovely world and we are to care for it. Planting a tree makes that part of the world more enjoyable and the air cleaner. Speak of being co-creators with God. Arrange a schedule for watering it during the next few months so that it will grow.

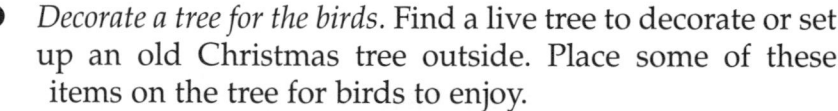

❿ *Decorate a tree for the birds.* Find a live tree to decorate or set up an old Christmas tree outside. Place some of these items on the tree for birds to enjoy.
- Lightly toast bread slices and cut in shapes to hang on tree. These may be spread with peanut butter.
- Tie a string around the upper part of a pine cone and spread hardened bacon grease on the remainder of the cone. Roll the greased section of the cone in birdseed, and tie it to the tree.
- String popcorn or cranberries and arrange them on the tree.
- Cut an orange and scoop out the pulp. String the pulp and hang on tree. Mix one part peanut butter to two parts birdseed and put mixture in scooped out orange half. Hang the orange half on tree.

❿ *Thank God for senses.* Place these items on a table and ask each family group to stop by the table to experience each of their senses and to thank God for their senses.
- **FEEL** cotton balls, sand, fuzzy toy
- **SMELL** spices, evergreen
- **HEAR** pebbles dropping, voices in a recording
- **SEE** nature items through magnifying glass
- **TASTE** apple slices

▶ *Build a snack.* Place various fruit items on a table. Family groups can work together to peel, chop, and prepare the food. Then have each person put together a snack with the fruits he or she likes. Talk about how God not only made different fruits, but God made each of us different, and we each enjoy different foods.

▶ *Explore textures.* Look at various textures that are found in nature. If you cannot go outside, bring some of the items indoors. Look at rough rocks and smooth stones. Feel various tree barks. Recognize that fresh corn is both smooth and rough in texture. Run your hands through sand, through heavy dirt, through clay and recognize the different types of soil that God created. Thank God for the sense of feeling.

▶ *Watch caterpillars and butterflies.* Arrange to watch caterpillars spin their chrysalis and change into butterflies. If you don't have a local source of butterflies, contact Insect Lore at 1-800-LIVE-BUG.

▶ *Grow plants.* Plant seeds and watch them grow or cut the tops off carrots and put them in a dish with shallow water. The carrot tops will sprout and grow lacey leaves.

▶ *Make butter.* Place cream in a quart jar and put the cap on tight. Shake the jar vigorously until butter begins to form. When the butter has formed well and the liquid looks watery, pour it out, collecting the butter and forming it into a lump. Enjoy the butter with crackers or bread. Thank God for butter.

▶ *God gives us growth.* Look up the following verses and discuss how God planned for us to continue to grow, even when we are adults. The verses may be paraphrased and/or illustrated. You may make these paraphrased verses into a litany by using the bold print between the verses as responses.

Genesis 1:31
Thank you, God, for your plan for growth.

Ecclesiastes 3:1
Thank you, God, that we grow from babies to adults.

Proverbs 17:17
Help us, God, to remember our friends.

Ephesians 4:32
We will try to use our actions to produce good feelings, dear God.

Ephesians 4:15
Our minds continue to grow, no matter what our age. Thank you, God.

Deuteronomy 4:35 b
We thank you, God, that we understand more about you each day. Thank you, God, for growth. Amen.

▶ *Investigate the world.* Place various items from nature on a worship table. Ask learners to pick up an item and hold it and later tell the group why that item reminds them of God. The items may also include pictures of rainbows, ice or snow, a butterfly, animals, and so on.

▶ *Take a walk in socks.* Bring old socks to class and put these over your shoes. Then take a walk through a weeded area, collecting seeds on your socks. Plant the socks, and water well! Watch the seeds collected on the socks grow. Thank God for the many ways we move seeds around.

▶ *Explore seeds.* Collect various seeds and display them on a table. As you look at the seeds, talk about how God places the growth possibility inside each seed, and it will put out roots and a stem and make a plant. Talk about how different seeds are carried about in different ways. Some stick to our socks or an animal's fur and are moved about. Some are like little helicopters and are lifted on the wind. Some move from place to place by water. Some are planted by squirrels and other animals.

▶ *Illustrate a hymn.* Select a hymn about nature from your hymnal and print it on a large paper. Invite the class members to illustrate the words around the edges of the paper.

▶ *Sing hymns.* Check the topical index in your hymnal for a topic such as "Nature" for songs such as:
"For the Beauty of the Earth"
"All Creatures of Our God and King"
"This Is My Father's World"
"Morning Has Broken"
"All Things Bright and Beautiful"

Lent:
a Time to Prepare

[**NOTE:** Because there are so many possibilities for celebrating Lent, I will simply list a variety of suggestions here under four different themes.]

SESSION ONE

LENT, A TIME WE REMEMBER

Focus: *To review and learn about Jesus' life.*

LEARNING AND WORSHIP OPPORTUNITIES

▶ Draw or paint pictures of favorite stories about Jesus. Afterwards, ask each person to show his or her picture and tell what story of Jesus it represents.

▶ Prepare a Lenten wreath with 1 white and 7 purple candles (one for each week plus Easter). An alternative to the wreath is to use a wooden cross as the candle base.

▶ Make personal Lenten journals to be written in throughout Lent.

▶ Make Lenten Palm Calendar (see Handout #8, instructions in Ash Wednesday session, page 46).

▶ Talk about why purple is used for Lent (for penitence and royalty) and discuss any Lenten activities that your church has.

▶ Read these scriptures to remember Jesus' life:
Luke 2:1-7	Matthew 4:18-22	Mark 11:7-10
Luke 2:25-32	Matthew 5:1-12	Mark 14:22-25
Luke 2:41-52	Luke 10:29-37	John 19:16-18
Mark 1:9-11	Matthew 20:29-34	Matthew 28:1-8

▶ Act out one or more stories from Jesus' life.

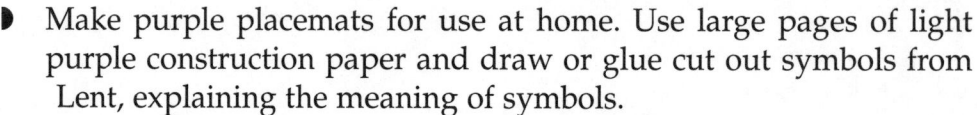

◗ Make purple placemats for use at home. Use large pages of light purple construction paper and draw or glue cut out symbols from Lent, explaining the meaning of symbols.

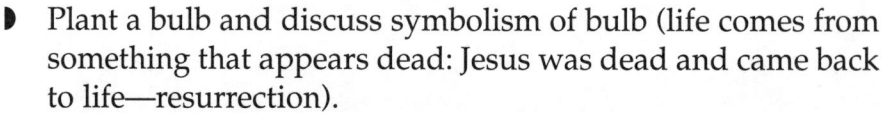

> ◗ Plant a bulb and discuss symbolism of bulb (life comes from something that appears dead: Jesus was dead and came back to life—resurrection).

> ◗ Using the scriptures listed on page 105, draw a mural of Jesus' life. Use any pictures drawn at beginning of session that illustrate any of the scriptures.

> ◗ Create "scripture sculptures" of a story about Jesus. (Decide on a scene from a story. Then have learners use their bodies in a fixed or statue position to depict the story scene. See pages 25 in chapter 4 for more directions.)

◗ For a worship time use hymns such as: "Tell Me the Stories of Jesus"; "We Would See Jesus"; "Joy to the World"; "I Love to Tell the Story."

◗ Create a story web: Stand in a circle with a ball of yarn. Pass the ball back and forth across the circle (with each person holding part of the yarn, unwinding the ball). When each person receives the yarn, he or she states, "I remember when Jesus. . . ." recalling one of the stories of Jesus. Close with a prayer of thanksgiving for Jesus. (Be sure everyone holds the yarn as you pray, even if they did not contribute a story.)

SESSION TWO

LENT, A TIME WE STUDY

Focus: *To recognize that Lent is a time for learning of our faith.*

LEARNING AND WORSHIP OPPORTUNITIES

◗ Make a cross. This can be made from craft sticks, pieces of wood, nails, or palm fronds. (See Ash Wednesday session, page 46.)

◗ Set up a display of crosses. Arrange ahead of time for persons to lend you a variety of types and styles of crosses for this display. It may be left up for a week or so for the congregation to view.

◗ Read Luke 2:41-52. Talk about how Jesus learned from his teachers and grew in wisdom.

▶ Read and discuss Matthew 6:1-4. **Ask: In what ways do we some-times act like this?**

▶ Learn about different styles of crosses, how they originated and the meaning behind them. (See Handout #7.)

▶ Paraphrase and illustrate Psalm 46:1-5 or Psalm 63:1-5 and/or 6-8 or Psalm 100.

▶ Make a wire cross to be filled with fresh flowers on Easter Sunday. To make the cross: shape hardware or chicken wire into cylinders forming the beams of a cross. (Or the wire may be wrapped loosely around the beams of a wooden cross). Flowers are then pushed into the wire. Ask learners to bring flowers for the cross, or contact a local florist for flowers they are about to discard.

▶ Use the trunk of old Christmas trees to form a rough cross to be used on Good Friday.

▶ Draw a symbol (other than a cross) that tells about your faith.

▶ For a worship time use hymns such as: "Old Rugged Cross"; "Lift High the Cross"; "In the Cross of Christ I Glory."

▶ Make Easter lilies by drawing around a hand on sheet of white paper. After cutting out hands, curl the "fingers" using a pencil. Then pull the two sides of the "palm" of the hand together, forming a lily. Use yellow construction paper for the center and green for leaves. Stand in a circle placing the Easter lilies in the center in the form of a cross.

▶ Talk about how Jesus felt so strong about what he believed about God that he would not compromise those beliefs and died on the cross instead. Pray a prayer of thanks for that example for us and ask God to help each to stand up for our beliefs.

SESSION THREE

LENT, A TIME WE PRAY AND FAST

Focus: *To discover why we pray and fast, and to experience these disciplines.*

LEARNING AND WORSHIP OPPORTUNITIES

▶ Look up and illustrate facts about world hunger. (Check the library and the web site www.thehungersite.com.)

▶ Count the number of water faucets in your house and read about water facts and water availability in economically struggling countries of the world. (For this, check the Handout #18 and the web site www.refugeecamp.org/degrade/water.)

▶ Read Matthew 6:5-15 and discuss prayer as talking to AND listening to God.

▶ Reread Matthew 6:11 and recognize that God does not want us to take more than our share of today's food. The Contemporary English Version of the Bible reads: "Give us our food for today."

▶ Read Matthew 6:16-18. Discuss fasting as a way to remember how Jesus suffered and others suffer today. Talk about what foods learners might give up for a period of time, or how they might decrease the amount they spend on one meal per week and give the money saved to someone in need.

▶ Make pretzels. (See page 45 in Ash Wednesday study for recipe.)

▶ Write letters to God. These may be taken home and used as prayers.

 ▶ Make and illustrate a banner or poster with Matthew 6:16-18 on it. Hang it near your table at home.

  ▶ Make "tent prayers" to be placed on the table at home. (Write or draw a prayer on the bottom end of a rectangular piece of card-weight paper. Fold the card in half to make a tent.)

  ▶ For a worship time use hymns such as: "Do Lord, Remember Me"; "Every Time I Feel the Spirit"; "Take Time to Be Holy."

 ▶ Write a prayer litany together. Use it during the session and arrange for its use in a congregational service.

▶ As families or individuals, decide on something you like that you will give up or some positive action you will add to your routine. Write these on paper butterflies, explaining the symbolism of the butterfly.

SESSION 4

LENT, A TIME WE ACT

Focus: *To decide on positive actions as Christians.*

LEARNING AND WORSHIP OPPORTUNITIES

▶ Kindness Tree - Anchor a branch in a bucket of sand or soil. Tie a few 3 x 5 cards on tree with ideas of acts of kindness. Ask persons to add cards to the tree with several kind acts they might do.

▶ Stand around the Kindness Tree and sing a hymn of discipleship and service. Ask each person to take a card from the tree that he or she can act on during the rest of Lent.

▶ Make Easter cards to send to friends or family.

▶ Make posters of joy to share in a nursing home or for shut-in members. Arrange for persons of various ages to deliver these.

▶ Read Romans 12:9-21.

▶ Read a story about someone learning to share or going out of his or her way to help others. *The Rainbow Fish* by Marcus Pfister and *Mufaro's Beautiful Daughters: An African Tale* by John Steptoe are good examples.

▶ Select a service project you will do as a group or in families. (See chapter 6 for ideas.)

▶ Plan an Easter drama for a Sunday school class or for worship.

▶ Visit a nursing home or a shut-in as a group.

▶ Plant signs. Make small signs with statements such as CHRIST IS RISEN—JESUS IS LORD—EASTER JOY—HE LIVES! Attach them to craft sticks and place them in the lawn on Easter morning.

▶ Plan a garden on the church property and arrange for tending it. Give the food that is grown to families in need.

▶ For a worship time use hymns such as: "Where He Leads Me"; "Here I Am, Lord"; "Whom Shall I Send?"; "Are Ye Able, Said the Master."

▶ Plan a time to have a "reunion" after Easter Sunday and talk about what you have each done to share Christ's message of caring. Thank God for this opportunity to remember, to study, to pray, and to prepare to act.

Prayer: Conversation with God

Focus: *To learn about prayer and experience praying together.*

Scripture: Matthew 6:9-13

LEARNING AND WORSHIP OPPORTUNITIES

▶ *Imaginary conversation.* Ask each learner to make up a person in their head that they will pretend to be. Think about what that person looks like; what sort of family he or she is from; what age and what sort of job he or she has or whether the person goes to school; and what he or she likes to do in leisure time. Divide the learners into pairs and ask them to introduce themselves to each other, pretending to be the imaginary person.

Next ask the pairs to imagine the following things about their imaginary person and tell one another. Give them only one assignment at a time to work with:

1. Tell of something happy that has just happened to you.
2. Tell of some sort of fear that you have as the imaginary person.
3. Tell the person of some problem your imaginary person needs help with.
4. Thank the other person for something nice that they might have given you as an imaginary person.

Say: *Prayer is something like your conversations you have been having. What did you do during your conversations?* (**Tell about self; share experiences; ask for help; thank the person**) *Did one person do all the talking? Prayer is having a conversation with God, but that means listening as well as talking.*

▶ *Litany on prayer.* Use the litany below about prayer. The learners can easily respond if you write the response on a chalkboard or large sheet of paper.

WAYS GOD TALKS TO US TODAY

Leader: Jesus spoke to Paul on the road to Damascus, and God also speaks to us today. God speaks through the Bible.

Group: We listen, God, as you talk.

Leader: Teachers and preachers tell us of God.

Group: We listen, God, as you talk.

Leader: God talks to us through parents and friends.

Group: We listen, God, as you talk.

Leader: We can hear God speak in the wind and in the quiet of the early morning.

Group: We listen, God, as you talk.

Leader: God is within me and talks to my inner self.

Group: Help me, God, to listen for you every day and at all times. Amen.[1]

▶ *Read about Brother Lawrence.* Read the section about Brother Lawrence in Handout #5. Discuss ways that we can pray by talking to God as we work, just as Brother Lawrence did.

▶ *Make prayer chains.* You will need construction paper of various colors, cut into strips of about 1 x 6 inches. Each person will write his or her name on as many strips as there are persons in the class. They may also add something special that they would like prayer for. These are then handed out to every person. Each person will make a prayer chain to take home, with a link for every person in the class. When they pray, they can read each person's name and remember that person in prayer.

▶ *Make "tent prayers"* to be placed on the table at home. Write or draw a prayer on the end of a rectangle piece of card-weight paper. Fold the card in half to make a tent.

▶ *Make prayer pockets.* For each person you will need an envelope that has not been used, crayons or felt tip markers, and strips of paper about 1 ½ by 5 inches.[2]

1. Delia Halverson, Grades 5-6 Teacher, Vacation Bible School, 1987 (Nashville: Graded Press), p. 48.
2. Delia Halverson, *Teaching Prayer in the Classroom* (Nashville: Abingdon Press, 1989), p. 51.

1. Seal the envelope and cut it open on one of the short sides. This cut side becomes the top of a "pocket."
2. Decorate the envelope so that it looks like a pocket, using symbols, flowers, words, and so on.
3. As you talk about what might be included in a prayer, learners are to write ideas on the strips of paper and place them in the Prayer Pocket. Young children may cut pictures from magazines and glue them onto the strips of paper. Special prayer requests may be written on the papers.
4. Tell the learners that they can add to the pockets at home or take out things that they no longer feel a need to pray about. Encourage them to place the Prayer Pockets in their Bibles or keep them near a place where they regularly pray.

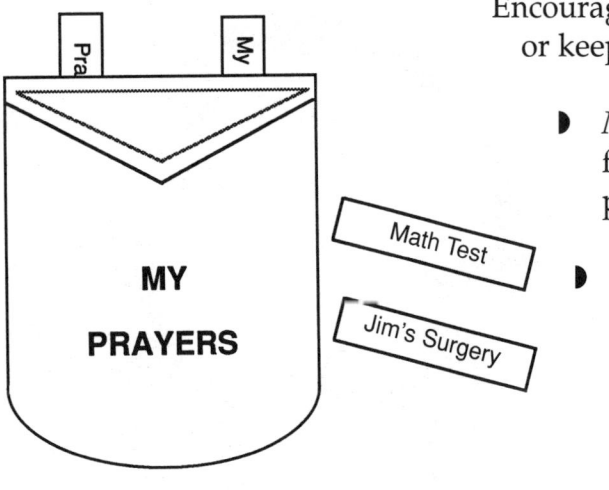

▶ *Make pretzels.* (See page 45 in Ash Wednesday study for recipe.) These symbolize the crossed arms in prayer.

▶ *Make prayer poem.* Create a *cinquain* poem using the format below. To create a group poem, first ask for suggestions of several words for each line of the poem. Then as a group choose the words to use in your poem. After you have created the group poem, you might have everyone work in smaller family groups to create prayer poems on their own. A sample poem appears below the instructions:

Line 1: A title of one word or one subject.
Line 2: Two words about the subject (either a phrase or separate words).
Line 3: Three verbs that denote action. These may end in "ing" or may be a phrase of action.
Line 4: Four words telling about the feeling for line one. May also be a phrase.
Line 5: One word that means the same as the first line (or reuse the first word or *Amen*).

Fear
Something new
Worrying, scary, upsetting
God, please help me.
Amen.

▶ *Make a devotional booklet.* Ask each family to write a devotion for a booklet. The form on Handout #17 will help them format the devotion. Make copies of the devotional booklet and give them to members of the church.

▶ *Devotional magazine.* Introduce a devotional magazine to the learners and ask them to divide into small groups to examine the magazine. Or ask one of the learners to read an item from the magazine to the class. If you are not familiar with any appropriate devotional magazines, write for samples of the following:

Pockets (magazine for children, appropriate for families of all ages).

Devo'Zine (magazine for youth, appropriate for families with youth)

Contact: Upper Room Publishers, P.O. Box 340004, Nashville, TN 37203-0004

▶ *Heritage Prayer.* Introduce some of the congregational prayers that you normally use in your corporate worship. Look for these in your denominational hymnal. Explain that these are common prayers that people have prayed for many years, and so we are praying them with a long line of witnesses to our faith.

▶ *Pray over snack.* Plan a snack of several things to enjoy during your session and ask persons to help you with a blessing. Tell them that you will open the prayer and then encourage persons to mention something on the table that they are thankful for. Let the responses come spontaneous instead of "going around the circle." Your opening might be something like the following.
Say: "There are many things for which we are thankful, God. Some of the things we are about to enjoy eating are. . . ." After the learners have mentioned items on the table, close with: "We thank you for all these things, our God. Amen."

▶ *Create litany.* A litany is a form of prayer, most often used in a group. In the litany, one or two lines are followed by a responsive phrase repeated by the entire group. This phrase is usually repetitive, although youth and children who read easily may enjoy some variation in the wording.

Children particularly enjoy litany prayers because they provide opportunity for verbal participation without the embarrassment of not knowing what to pray. When the litany is written by the children, they know the words before they offer the prayer. This takes away any pressure of thinking about what to say.

Use the central theme for the litany as the title. As ideas on the theme of the litany are offered, write them on a large piece of paper or on a chalkboard. Then agree on a response. You may use scripture passages or a phrase from a song as the response. Write this on a separate paper. Organize the ideas into some sort of pattern. Cut the statements apart and arrange them in order.

You may want to write a sentence of introduction for the worship leader, although it is not necessary. Use the litany as a prayer immediately and then again in your closing worship. Tape strips with the statements together for reading, with the understanding that there is a response between each statement.

Use the names or initials of each student beside his or her contribution. When the litany is used, ask each to read his or her own contribution.

The litany is not a performance, even when used before other people. Use simple language, even conversational tone so that learners look on prayer as a conversation with God.[3]

▶ *Sing prayer hymns.* Look in your hymnals in the topical index for prayer hymns. These might include:
> "Lord, Speak to Me"
> "Have Thine Own Way, Lord"
> "For the Beauty of the Earth"
> "Joyful, Joyful, We Adore Thee"
> "O Master, Let Me Walk with Thee"
> "Lord, I Want to Be a Christian"
> "Lord, We Come to Ask Your Blessing"
> "Bind Us Together, Lord"

▶ *Sing responses and blessings.* Your hymnals will also have responses and blessings that you frequently sing in your church. Use these. Some may include:
> "Be Present at Our Table, Lord"
> "Glory Be to the Father" (Gloria Patri)
> "Praise God, from Whom All Blessings Flow" (Doxology)
> "God Be in My Head" (Sarum Primer)
> "Lord, Have Mercy Upon Us" (Kyrie Eleison)*
> "Lord, Listen to Your Children Praying"*
> "Lord, Be Glorified"*
> "Father, I Adore You"*
> "Halle, Halle, Halleluja"*

3. Ibid., pp. 50-51.

*In *The Faith We Sing*, Pew Edition (Nashville: Abingdon Press, 2000).

Symbols: What Do They Mean?

Focus: *To help growth in appreciation of the cycle of special celebrations in our community of faith, including the colors, symbols, and other visual aids used at those times.*

Scriptures: See scriptures on Handout #10

LEARNING AND WORSHIP OPPORTUNITIES

▶ Make name tags using symbols of rainbow, star, dove, fish, candle, bread, chalice, cross, and flame as patterns.

▶ Bring resource books into the classroom or use the Internet to research other symbols that are found in your church building.

▶ Divide into eight family groups. (If your class is small, use four groups and give each two assignments.) Assign a scripture from Handout #10 to each group. Ask them to read the scripture in their groups and decide what symbol comes from that passage.

▶ Use symbols to make worship table coverings to be used at home. Give each household a white fabric about a yard square. The symbols may be drawn on the fabric with crayons and then ironed on the wrong side to help them stay intact during washing. You may also use fabric paints.

▶ Make a collage of symbols, using as many symbols as you can think of. Each person can design a symbol on a piece of paper, and then these can be mounted on a posterboard at various angles.

◗ Look for hymns in your hymnal that speak of various symbols in the words. These might be:

Angels	"Angels We Have Heard on High"
Bread	"Break Thou the Bread of Life"
	"Let Us Break Bread Together"
Bulb	"In the Bulb There Is a Flower"
Cross	"Jesus, Keep Me Near the Cross"
	"Lift High the Cross of Christ"
Eagle	"And God Will Raise You Up on Eagle's Wings"
Fire/Flame	"It Only Takes a Spark"
Hands	"He Touched Me"
Lamp	"Thy Word Is a Lamp Unto My Feet"
Rock	"Rock of Ages"
Sea	"There's a Wideness in God's Mercy Like the Wideness of the Sea"
Shepherd	"Jesus Like a Shepherd Lead Me"
	"The King of Love My Shepherd Is"
Trinity	"Holy, Holy, Holy" (. . . God in three persons, blessed Trinity)

◗ Ask each person to take a sheet of the colored construction paper and spend some time looking at the color and thinking about it. Then ask them to write on the paper any "feelings" that came to mind while they looked at the color. Come together and ask learners to share their feelings about the colors. Tell them that colors are ways that we express our feelings and certain colors help to bring about certain feelings. In this way, colors are symbols.

  ◗ Use Handout #10 to discuss the colors of the church year.

  ◗ Introduce the word "paraments" (altar and pulpit cloths used since the sixth century) and explain how churches use the colors to remind us of the seasons.

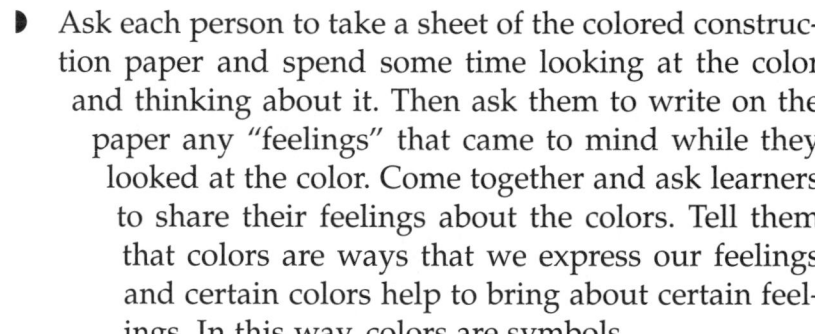

◗ Take a show-me trip through the sanctuary. If you have a large class, divide into family groups. Ask the class to look for symbols in the decorations, in the windows and furniture, and in the architecture. Ask them to look specifically for items with three or four parts, circles, and cross shapes. Explain that stained glass windows were used as reminders of Bible stories when most people could not read. Anything with three parts reminds us of the *trinity* (God as Father, Son, and Holy Spirit, three but one) and anything with four parts reminds us of the *four Gospels*. A circle reminds us that *God's love has no end*, and a dome or arches remind us that *God is over all the earth*. Come back together and ask each group to share their findings. Add additional information about these symbols and any other symbols as time allows.

▶ As the following information is read, have different persons use the named items to set up a worship center.

- The **white cloth** reminds us that we celebrate Christ coming into the world and his resurrection.
- The **purple ribbon** reminds us that we consider God as supreme ruler of our lives and that we are sorry for the times we act wrongly.
- The **green ribbon** reminds us of the way the news of God's love has spread and of ways we must grow in our own faith.
- The **red ribbon** reminds us that we must be on fire for Christ and allow the Holy Spirit to work in us.
- The **empty cross** reminds us that although Jesus had to die, God wouldn't let Jesus stay dead.
- The **Bible** reminds us that we must look to God's Word for direction.
- The **lighted candle** reminds us that Christ is among us and we must take the light to others. When two candles are lighted, we remember that Christ was both human and divine.

Worship: We Praise and Celebrate

Focus: *To help children and parents look at congregational worship as a celebration of God's love through action in which they participate, and to introduce them to our plan for action, the order of worship.*

Scriptures: Deuteronomy 31:12; Psalm 98

LEARNING AND WORSHIP OPPORTUNITIES

▶ On large sheet of paper, ask learners to draw pictures of the parts of the worship service each likes best. (These may later be mounted on a wall in the church.)

　▶ Get acquainted by having each person give their name and talk about their drawings.

　　▶ Read Deuteronomy 31:12, and talk about how God told Moses to gather all of the people, children included.

　　　▶ In groups, talk about times their family comes together for meals, special events, and so on.

　　　▶ Define "congregation" as a gathering of people.

　　　▶ Divide into groups of 5-6 persons (keeping parents and children together) to talk about times the church family comes together. Then as a whole group list those times.

　　　▶ Ahead of time, make a guide for worship appropriate to your own worship service. Use the information printed below as a guide. Print this off as a handout for families to use in the future. During the session, discuss the various definitions of the acts of worship, answering any questions.

DEFINITIONS FOR ACTS OF WORSHIP

PRELUDE . . . . We prepare for worship. Listen to the music and think of God's love.

LIGHTING THE CANDLES . . . . The light is brought to the altar to remind us that the living Christ is with us.

AFFIRMATION OF FAITH/CREED . . . . We say what we believe.

HYMN OF PRAISE . . . . We stand and sing joyfully to God.

PRAYER OF CONFESSION . . . . We think of things about our life we would like to change and ask God to help us.

PASTORAL PRAYER . . . . We ask God to be with us and with others who have special needs.

THE LORD'S PRAYER . . . . We pray the prayer that Jesus taught us.

GLORIA PATRI . . . . We sing a very old song of praise.

OFFERTORY . . . . We enjoy music as we give back to God some of what is given to us.

DOXOLOGY . . . . We sing praise to God for all we have.

MINISTRY OF MUSIC . . . . This special music praises God, and sometimes God talks to us through the music.

SCRIPTURE . . . . We hear God's Word from the Bible.

MESSAGE/SERMON . . . . We hear the pastor explain God's Word and what God wants us to do.

HYMN TO CLOSE . . . . We dedicate (promise) to do God's work.

CARRYING OUT THE LIGHT . . . . The symbol of the living Christ is taken into the world, leading us as we take God's love to others.

BENEDICTION . . . . The pastor sends us out into the world to care.

CHORAL/CONGREGATIONAL RESPONSE . . We sing that God's love is through all the world, and we will take it to others.

POSTLUDE . . . . Music plays, sending us out to take God to others.

▶ Prior to the session, make a poster of the following symbols and action words:

O Sing   **C** Hear   **/** Pray   **=** Respond.

Tell the class that there is actually a lot of action going on in our congregational worship. Hand out bulletins or a copy of the order of worship

---

you usually use, and ask the parents and children to work together placing the symbols from the poster (sing, hear, pray, or respond) beside each item on the bulletin. Some items may need two symbols. Be sure that the symbol for "respond" is used for the offertory and benediction.

▶ Practice reading the Lord's Prayer together.

▶ Look at the various indexes in your hymnal. Look up hymns in several of the indexes, particularly in the scripture index.

▶ Hand out index cards and explain how reading hymns is different from most reading. Practice singing, using the index cards to follow the lines.

▶ Look at various creeds in your hymnal. Read together a creed that you often use in worship. Remind the class that some of these creeds were written hundreds of years ago and we still believe them today.

▶ Write a creed. Ask persons to write just what they believe using a few words. Encourage them to share these creeds with others.

▶ Look at the membership vows that your members take. These vows may be in your worship hymnal. If not, get a copy of them for the class to use. Talk about ways that we can carry out those vows.

▶ Create a worship center. (See the session on symbols and colors on page 115.) Light the candle and remind everyone that this symbolizes Christ with us. Explain that the colors on the worship center are those used at different times of the year in worship.

▶ Have Psalm 98 read.

▶ Pray a litany prayer by asking each person to mention a part of the worship service, after which everyone responds, "We thank you, God." As the leader, begin with "We thank you, God, that you have called us to worship you together as a church family." After all have shared, end with "We know that you made us, and we worship you. Amen."

▶ Give each family a copy of the Lord's Prayer and a candle. Ask them to practice the Lord's Prayer during the week and to light their candle from the Christ candle, taking it home with them. (They may want to extinguish it outside for safety reasons.) Suggest that they use the candle at home for brief times of worship.

▶ Sing "Holy, Holy, Holy," "Joyful, Joyful, We Adore Thee," "We Gather Together," "Come, Christians, Join to Sing," "All Hail the Power of Jesus' Name," or another song of praise.

Part 4

HANDOUTS

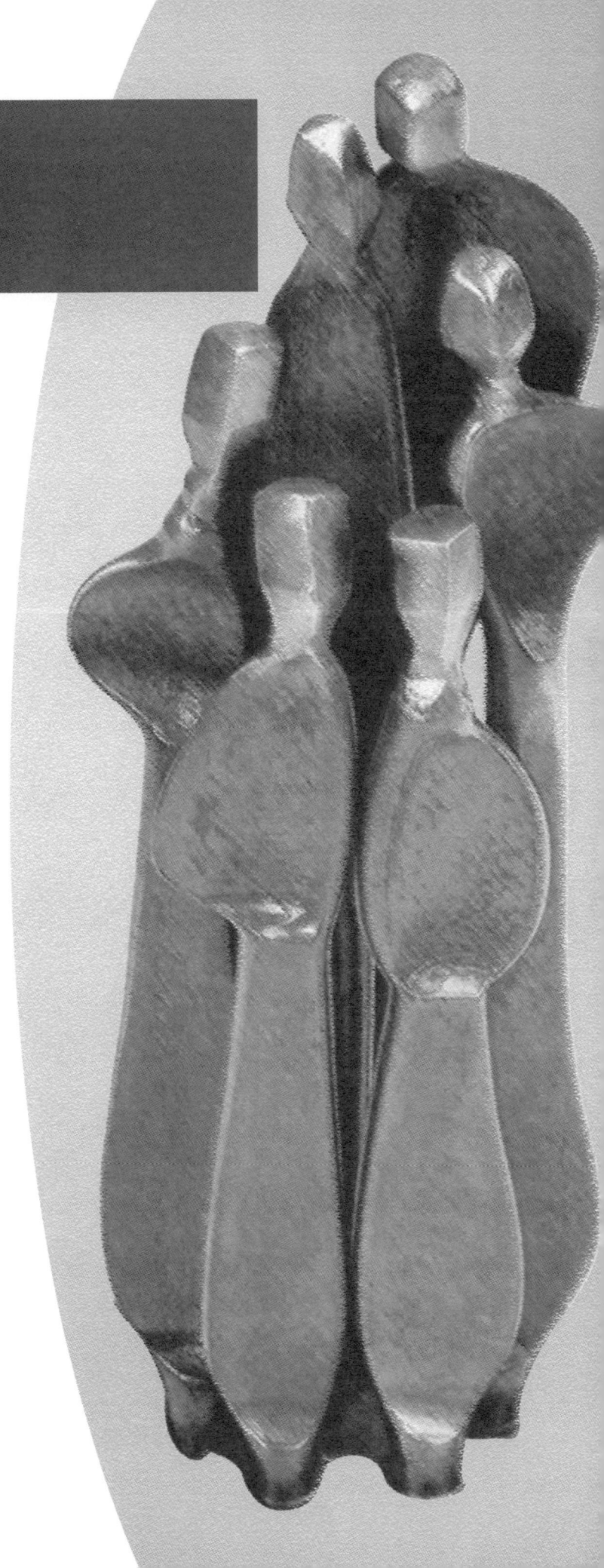

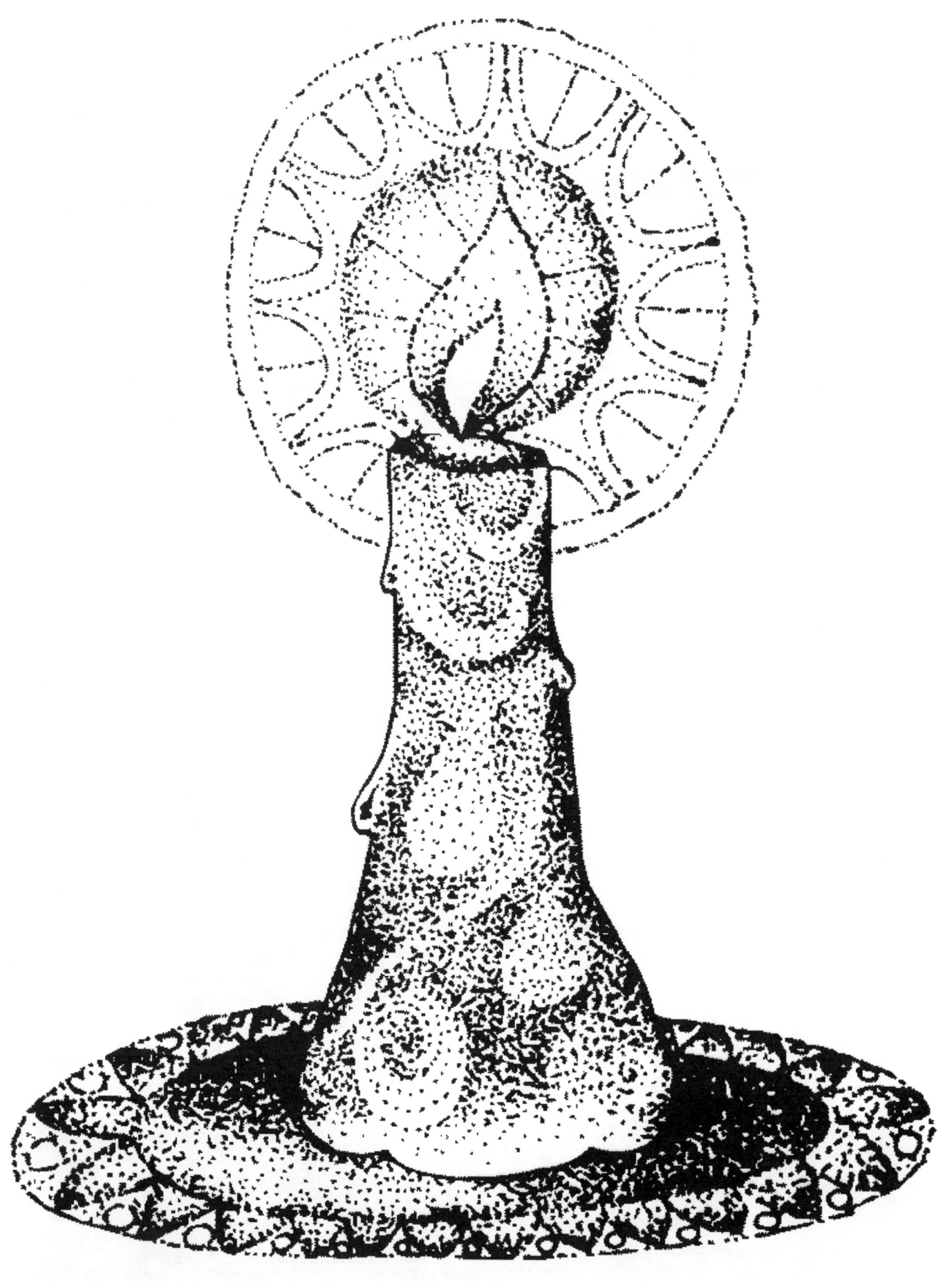

Advent Chain

Advent is a time when we prepare for Christmaas, our celebration of Christ's birth. Cut apart the sections below. Using glue or tape, connect the two ends into links, threading each link into another, forming a chain. Each day of December, prior to Christmas, read and follow the directions on the appropriate link.

December 1—Read Isaiah 11:1-2*a*
Prepare for Christmas by telling a favorite story about Jesus.

December 2—Read Luke 10:29-37
In this story Jesus tells us who our neighbor is. Think of someone you know who may be lonely and make some cookies or something else good to eat and take it to the person.

December 3—Read Mark 10:43*b*-44
Find something that you can do for others without letting them know that you are doing it. Remember, keep your identity a secret!

December 4—Read Mark 1:35
Jesus found a place where he could be alone to pray. Find a place in your house or yard where you can go alone and pray to God. Your prayer doesn't have to be long. Just say something like, "God, I'm here and I want to talk with you." Then tell God whatever is happening in your life this week.

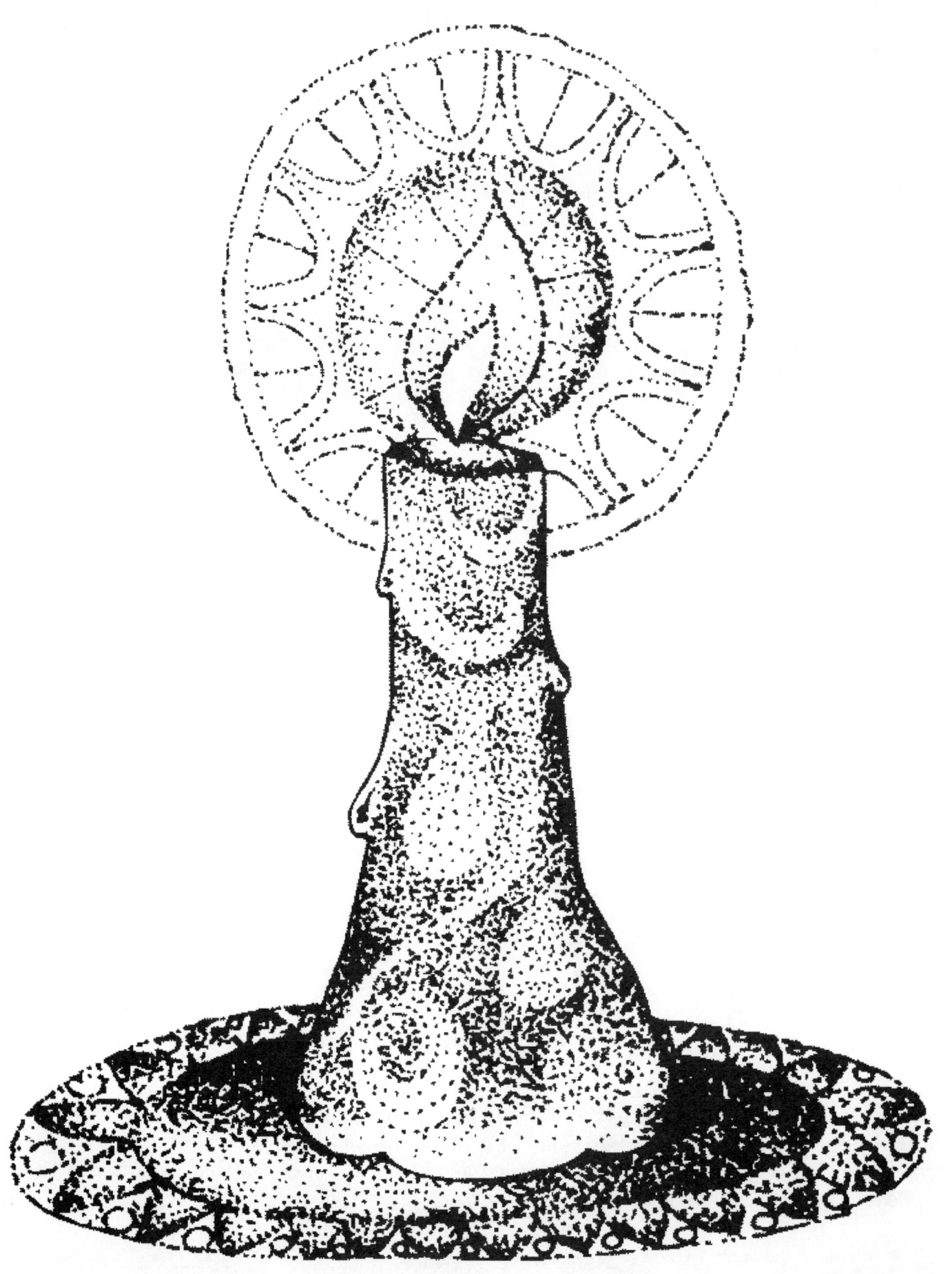

December 5—Read Mark 10:13-14

Select a toy that you have that is in good condition, or purchase a new one, and give it to an agency in town that collects toys for children at Christmas.

December 6—Read John 8:31-32

Jesus told us to know what is true. Make "tent notes" to go on your table for meals. Do this by folding 3 x 5 cards in half and writing some truths that you know on them. These truths might be something like, "God loves me every day." "I can depend on God to bring the rains to make plants grow." "Jesus wants me to love even those who hate me."

December 7—Read Matthew 6:9-13

Jesus taught us a prayer to use. Pray the Lord's Prayer at the end of the day today.

December 8—Read Mark 1:16-19

Jesus asked twelve men to be special followers (or disciples) of his. Jesus also wants us to follow him. When you follow someone, you do as that person does. List things that you can do that will show that you are a follower (or disciple) of Jesus.

December 9—Read Matthew 25:35-36

Jesus said that when we do things for others in his name, it is as if we are doing it for him. Decide on something you can do for someone else, such as helping to serve at a soup kitchen or going through your clothes and giving away some of your better clothes for someone who doesn't have good clothes.

December 10—Read Mark 12:29-30

When we love someone, we like to do something for them. Think of something that you (and your family) can do for your church. It may be to pick up trash on the grounds, to pick up bulletins after a service, or to help take a basket of food to someone. Make arrangements at church to do this.

December 11—Read Mark 12:31

Make a greeting card for someone you know who lives far away. Tell them that you love them and God loves them. Send the card in the mail.

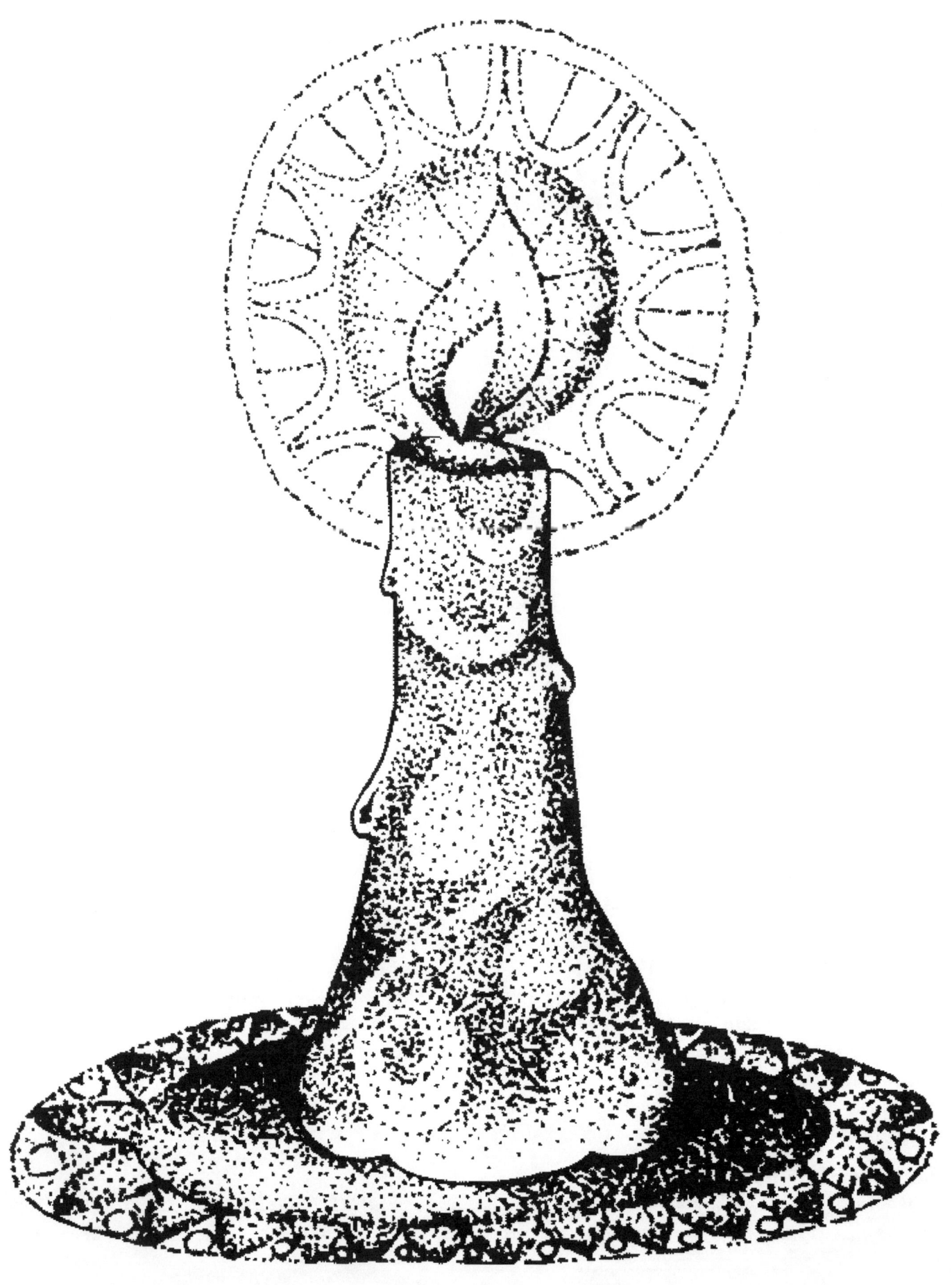

December 12—Read John 8:12

Remember that following Jesus is like having a light to show the way. After dark, close all the shades in your house and turn out all of the lights for a few minutes. While the lights are out, look at your hands and feet. Try walking a short distance in the dark. Then turn on the lights and see how much easier it is to walk.

December 13—Read Matthew 5:13

Jesus said that we are to make a difference in life, just as salt makes a difference in the taste of things. Cook something without salt and taste the difference in the food before adding salt to it.

December 14—Read Matthew 18:21-22

Jesus told us to forgive others many, many times. Think of someone who has done something wrong to you. Write a letter to that person saying that you forgive him or her.

December 15—Read Matthew 5:14-16

Jesus said that we should let others see that we love God and follow God's way, just like a lamp must not be hidden in order to show its light. Light a candle in a dark room. Then cover it with a large metal bowl or pot. Notice the difference. What happens to the light of the candle?

December 16—Read Luke 15:3-6

We sometimes call Jesus the Good Shepherd. The shepherd cares for his sheep. Find pictures of sheep in magazines and on Christmas cards and make a collage by gluing the pictures of the sheep onto a large piece of paper that you can hang in your home.

December 17—Read Luke 17:11-19

This is the story of how Jesus healed ten men of a terrible disease, but only one came back to thank him. Write a thank-you note for someone who has done something nice for you. Tell them in the note that God loves them and you love them too.

December 18—Read John 8:1-11

It was the custom in that day to stone a woman who slept with a man besides her husband. Jesus told those who had come to stone the woman that the person who had not sinned should throw the first stone. Find a rock and write on it "1st stone" and keep it to remind you that we all do things we know we shouldn't do and so we must not accuse others.

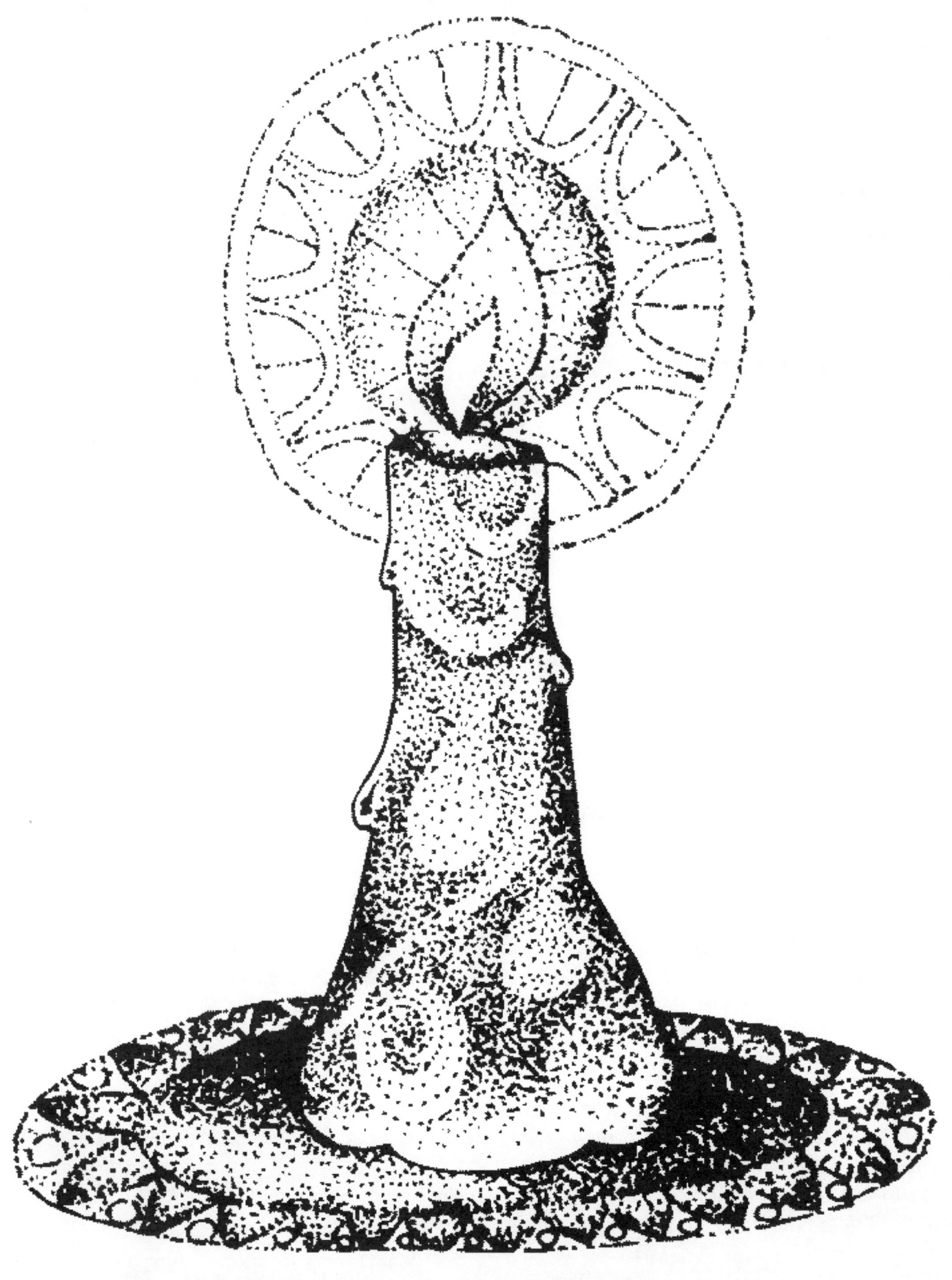

December 19—Read John 14:27
Jesus came to bring peace. Peace is when people work together for the good of all. Look at Christmas cards or in magazines for pictures that remind us of peace. Select one picture about peace and glue it on construction paper. Make a hole in the top of the picture and hang it somewhere so that you can see it every day to remind you of why Jesus came.

December 20—Read John 15:5
We sometimes use the symbol of the vine and its branches to remind us of Jesus. Look around outside for a vine that may be growing near your house. Look at the bottom of the vine to where it is rooted in the ground. Write a reminder to yourself to watch the vine in the weeks ahead and see how it grows and how the branches grow.

December 21—Read John 6:1-12
Jesus cared about the people when they were hungry. Make some bread rolls or biscuits to give to someone who is hungry. Put it in a little basket or wrap it in a nice cloth. Put the scripture reference with the bread.

December 22—Read Luke 2:1-7
Mary and Joseph traveled a long distance to Bethlehem. It was about 80 miles. Find a place on the map that is about 80 miles from your town. Talk about what it would be like to walk that far.
Sing together: "Silent Night, Holy Night."

December 23—Read Luke 2:8-20
The angels came to tell the shepherds about the special person that was born in Bethlehem.
Sing together: "While Shepherds Watched Their Flocks by Night."

December 24—Read Matthew 2:1-7
The Magi (or wise men) saw a star in the east and followed it. Make a star and hang it in your home. Look at the Christmas decorations in your home and around town and count the number of stars you see. These remind us of the special person that the Magi traveled hundreds of miles to see.

December 25—Read Matthew 2:8-12
The Magi (or wise men) brought gifts for the Baby Jesus. At Christmas we give gifts to each other and remember that God gave us Christ, the best gift of all. Write notes of thanks to those who gave you gifts. In the notes remind them of God's gift, the Baby Jesus.

From *Side by Side: Families Learning and Living the Faith Together*, by Delia Halverson. Copyright © 2002 by Abingdon Press. Reproduced by permission.

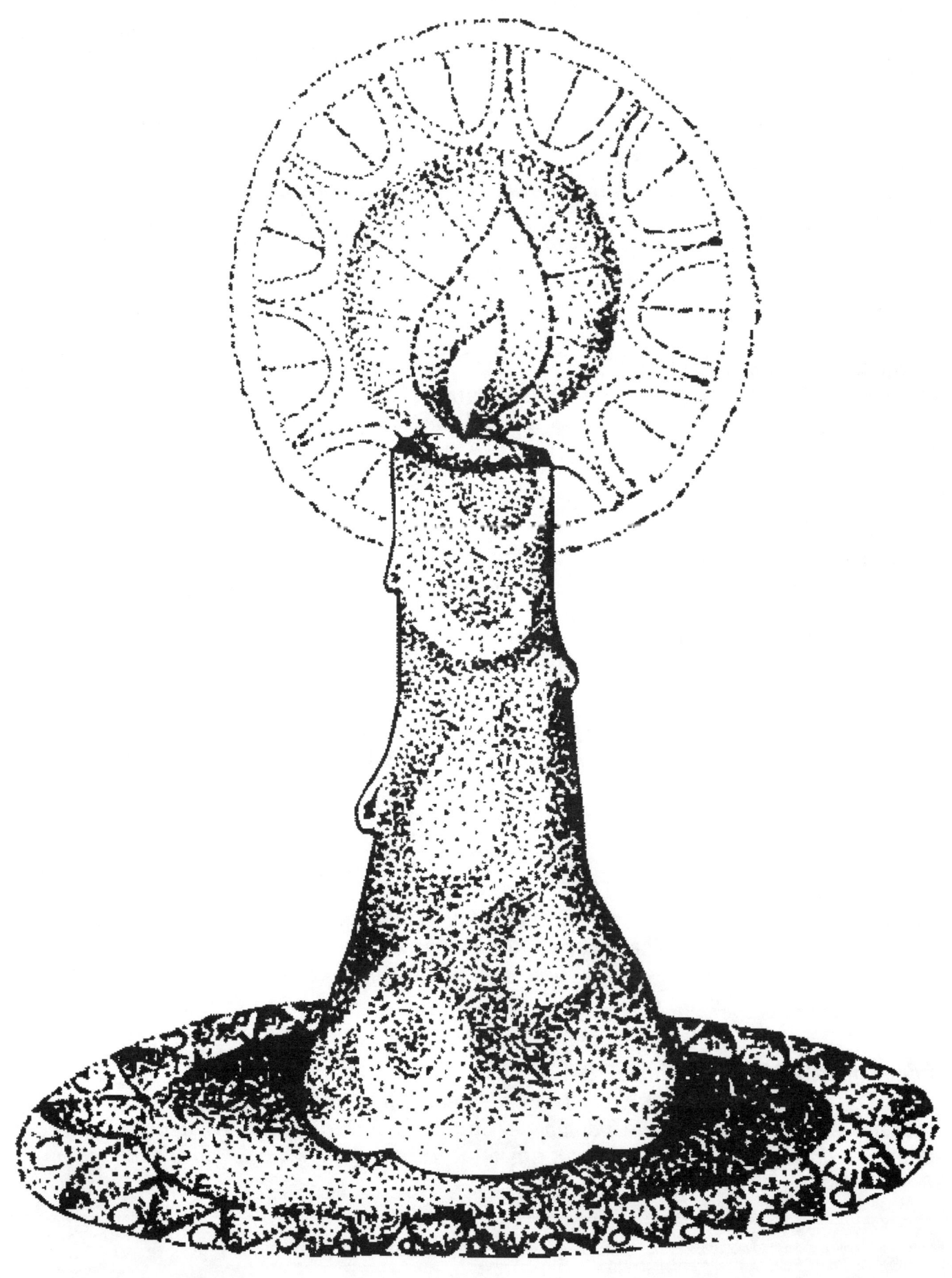

Advent Wreath

The Advent wreath is used to help us prepare for Christmas, our celebration of the coming of Christ.

- The circle stands for God's love that is with us always.
- The evergreens symbolize everlasting life.
- The four candles represent the four weeks of Advent.
- The color purple is used to remind us to prepare by recalling the things we've done that are not good and to change our lives.

Read the scripture below and light candles one by one—one for each week that goes by.

WONDER   Week 1: Isaiah 11:1-2*a*

Centuries ago, people thought God was very distant. They only thought of God in fear and among the clouds above. They thought God zapped them when they did wrong. The prophets helped them see God in a new way, and Jesus came to show us what God is really like. We wonder at such a personal God.

> *Prayer: Our God, we begin to prepare for the coming of the Christ Child and our hearts and lives are filled with wonder and praise. As we talk and work with each other during these weeks, help us to remember how Jesus taught us to love one another. Amen.*

JOY   Week 2: Luke 2:4-14

Joy is something we often feel as we prepare for Christmas. Perhaps it is because of all the fun things that happen during these days. We need to also think about the joy that comes from knowing that Jesus came into this world to make it a better place for us and to help us understand what God is like.

> *Prayer: Our God, our hearts are filled with joy and gladness as we spend this week preparing for our celebration of Jesus' birth. Help us to share that joy with others wherever we may go. Amen.*

GENEROSITY   Week 3: Luke 2:15-20

Too often, at Christmas, we only think of what we will receive. People ask, "What do you want for Christmas?" or they say, "What did you get for Christmas?" This makes us think only of "getting." But the custom of giving and receiving gifts should remind us to give. As you buy or make gifts for Christmas, think about just how the person who receives the gift will feel. What sort of expression will be on his or her face when the gift is opened? How will the gift be used?

Prayer: Our God, as we make or buy gifts for others, we remember that Christ was your gift to the world. Help us to live the life that Jesus taught us, always loving others as much as ourselves. Amen.

LOVE   Week 4: John 3:16

We use the word love in so many different ways. We say we love a person, we love pizza, we love to go to the beach. The Greeks had four different words for love. A friendship love was called *philos*. The name of the city Philadelphia comes from this word. A sexual love was called *eros*. Our word erotic comes from this. The love that God has for us is *charis* (kah-ris). We translate that into English as "grace." God loves us with a happy heart and sometimes with a sad heart, but God always has "grace" or *charis*. The love that we have for God as we respond to God's love is *agape*. This love causes us to do good to others and act in the way that God wants us to act. When we have *agape* love we help to bring peace to the world.

Prayer: Our God, we thank you for the love that Jesus taught us. Help us to spread that love wherever we go. We know that love brings about peace. May we help to bring that about. Amen.

132

Christmas Symbols

Use these Christmas symbols with Advent 2 lesson, page 51. Reproduce and trace them onto light card stock and cut them out to be used as stencils for tracing. If you have the capability, enlarge the symbols for easier use.

Star

Manger

Crown

Lamb

Angel

Wreath

Dove

Candle

134

The Story Behind the Christmas Carol

"O COME, O COME, EMMANUEL"   *Isaiah 11:1-3*

The roots of this carol go back as far as the ninth century or earlier. That early version was based on seven antiphons (where two groups respond back and forth). These all began with "O," using many of the terms for the Messiah in the Scripture. They are Wisdom, Lord, Root of Jesse, Key of David, Orient, King, and God-with-us (or Emmanuel). In the twelfth century, a Latin antiphon was written that used five of these themes. Then in 1851 John Mason Neale paraphrased into English the twelfth century words. He put them to a melody that was sung by a community of French Franciscan nuns in the fifteenth century.

And so this carol has come down to us through the centuries, being adjusted and adapted at various times. But it still gives us great joy to sing it when we prepare ourselves for Christmas.

"O LITTLE TOWN OF BETHLEHEM"   *Luke 2:1-6*

In 1865 an Episcopal minister, Phillips Brooks, went on a visit to the Holy Land. He decided to take a horseback ride from Jerusalem to Bethlehem in order to be there for the celebration of Christ's birthday. As it got dark on Christmas Eve, he was riding through a field where tradition says the shepherds were keeping their flocks. He visualized the scene that went into his carol: the little town in the distance with stars shining above, one star brighter than the rest. Three years later, back in Philadelphia, he thought of this scene as he prepared for Christmas. He wrote a poem for the children in his church to recite and asked his church organist, Lewis Redner, to compose music to go with it. The tune didn't come to Mr. Redner's mind until he awoke in the middle of the night before the Sunday school program. The children sang the song for the first time almost 130 years ago.

The words remind us of the ordinary world that Jesus came to with an extraordinary message.

"SILENT NIGHT, HOLY NIGHT"   *Luke 2:6-7*

According to one story, out of the simplicity of an Austrian band of roving actors, performing in 1818, came the inspiration for this song. It began when the mice ate the bellows of the church organ and the actors' annual presentation of the Christmas story had to be held in a home. On his way home the assistant pastor, Josef Mohr, reflected on the real meaning of Christmas as he walked over a small hill and looked down on the village below. Another story says that Mohr had just been to a village home to baptize a baby when he returned and looked down from the hill on the village below. Whatever the occasion, a poem began to form in his head, and he wrote it down as soon as he got home.

The next day Mohr rushed the verses over to the church organist, Franz Gruber, and asked him to set it to music. On Christmas Day the organ still did not work, but Gruber accompanied the congregation in singing the carol for the first time. A few weeks later when the organ repairman arrived and finished fixing the organ, Gruber sat down and played the piece. The repairman took the song back to his own village where a family of Austrian singers began singing it. They became famous and the song spread to become a European favorite. It was translated into English in 1863 by Jane Campbell.

This carol has become one of the most loved carols in the world, and as Franz Gruber's wife said, "We will die, you and I, but this song will live."

"AWAY IN A MANGER"   *Luke 2:7*

"Away in a Manger" may have been the first Christmas carol you learned. It is a favorite among children everywhere. The author of the words is unknown, but it was put to music in America in the late 1800s by James R. Murray. Some versions of the song call it "Luther's Cradle Hymn," probably because Luther used to sing his children to sleep with lullabies. It is believed that it may have first been sung among the German people living in Pennsylvania.

The words of this song bring to our minds just what it may have been like on the night over two thousand years ago when Jesus was born.

"The Remarkable Story Behind 'Silent Night'" by Lindsay Terry, (Ed) Peter Batzing. American Tract Society, P. O. Box 462008, Garland, Texas 75046. Used by Permission.

"HARK! THE HERALD ANGELS SING"
Luke 2:10-14; 2 Corinthians 5:19

Charles Wesley, the brother to the founder of Methodism, John Wesley, wrote at least 6,500 hymns. This is one of his best known, and it was written less than a year after his conversion in 1738. The original words were "Hark, how the welkin rings, Glory to the new-born King." Wesley, himself, realized that the word "welkin" (which means heavens or sky) was an archaic term and so he changed it in 1753. Each line of the carol has deep theological meaning.

Wesley set this carol to different music than we use today. Our music today comes from a festive choral work that Felix Mendelssohn wrote in 1840 for the four-hundredth anniversary of the invention of the printing. It was not until fifteen years later, after Mendelssohn's death, that an English musician put Wesley's words to his second chorus of the choral work.

The carol not only tells the story of the shepherds' encounter with the angels, but brings deep understanding of Christian spirituality.

"GO, TELL IT ON THE MOUNTAIN"   Luke 2:6-20

The chorus of this song was an African American spiritual. In the mid-1900s John Wesley Work, Jr., an instructor at Fisk University, an African American university in Nashville, Tennessee, was also director of the Fisk Jubilee Singers, a well-known chorus that taught the world to sing the spirituals. When he heard the chorus to this song, he wrote the melody and words for the stanzas.

Each Christmas, around 5:00 A.M., the students and faculty of Fisk would walk around campus singing Christmas songs. This was one of their favorites. After the early morning singing, they would gather in the dining hall where they found brightly decorated tables and glowing candles. There they had a brief Christmas service followed by breakfast. Today this spiritual is translated into many languages and loved around the world.

The song calls Christians to proclaim this special birth of a Savior from the higher point of the mountain.

"WE THREE KINGS"   *Matthew 2:1-12*

This hymn is unique in that both the words and the music were written by the same person. Some people even consider this the first "All-American" carol. It was written in 1857 by John Henry Hopkins, Jr., an Episcopalian rector.

This is one of the few carols we have that are based on legend, such as the term "kings" for the wise men and the reference to a specific number of these prestigious visitors.

The carol helps us to tell the story according to Matthew's Gospel.

"JOY TO THE WORLD"

Psalm 98:4-9

Isaac Watts, the writer of this hymn, began writing poems at the age of seven. The story is told that as a youth he was very disturbed that none of the songs sung at church were joyful and his parents challenged him to write one that was, and so he wrote "Joy to the World." The hymn does not speak of the usual images associated with Christmas, and so it is appropriate to be sung at any time of the year. The hymn was sung to a variety of tunes for over 100 years before Lowell Mason, a New England music teacher, put it to the tune we have today. There are two musical phrases in the hymn influenced by George Frideric Handel's *Messiah*.

Another story about Watts tells of his invitation to spend a week visiting friends, and the week expanded to 36 years! His hostess of 36 years, however, declared that his visit was "the shortest" she had ever experienced.

Isaac Watts is called the father of English Hymnody and is honored by a memorial in Westminster Abbey. We know of 454 songs in use today that he wrote. He published 52 volumes of hymns and songs.

This song expresses praise of Jesus Christ in unsurpassed joy. We cannot help expressing that joy as we sing it.

Used by permission. *Creative Ideas for Advent, Vol. 1* (Prescott, Arizona: Educational Ministries, Inc.), p. 47.

Past and Present Saints

SO GREAT A CROWD OF WITNESSES!

Leader: Faith is living in relationship with God. Our ancestors in the faith lived with God.

#1 We remember Abraham and Sarah who had faith enough to move to a new country.

#2 We remember Joseph who believed in God even when he was taken from his home.

#3 We remember Jochebed, the mother who saved her son, Moses, in fear of her life, and her daughter, Miriam, who watched over Moses.

#4 We remember Moses who had difficulty speaking but still led his people to freedom.

All: **These are saints of the past.**

#1 We remember David and Esther, royal leaders who loved God.

#2 We remember Samuel and Deborah, prophets who spoke for God.

#3 We remember Mary and Joseph, simple people who followed God's calling.

All: **These are saints of the past.**

#1 We remember the disciples of Jesus.

#2 We remember the writers of the Gospels.

#3 We remember early church leaders, like Paul and Lydia, Barnabas and Priscilla.

All: **For all these saints of the past, we give you thanks, O God. Amen.**

From *Side by Side: Families Learning and Living the Faith Together*, by Delia Halverson. Copyright © 2002 by Abingdon Press. Reproduced by permission.

FOLD

ST. FRANCIS OF ASSISI

Francis was happy as a boy in the house of his rich father. He had no need to work like the children in poor families, and he dreamed dreams of being richer than his father and leading a thousand men in the military. By the time he was 25 he had his riches. Francis had everything money could buy, but he was not happy. He joined the military, but became seriously ill and was discharged as a failure.

Back in Assisi, Francis walked the streets to a part of town he'd never seen before. People were hungry, dressed in smelly rags, covered with sores. At least, he thought, I can help these people. As he helped them he became happy. Then he thought, if I become happy doing these little things, how much happier if I live exactly as God wants me to live? Soon his love for God overflowed into a love for all of God's creation, nature and people. He wrote his feelings in prayers and poems, many of which we enjoy today. Here is one.

Lord, make me an instrument of your peace.
Where there is hatred, let me sow love;
Where there is injury, pardon;
Where there is doubt, faith;
Where there is despair, hope;
Where there is darkness, light;
And where there is sadness, joy.

O, Divine mMaster, grant that I may not so much seek to be consoled, as to console;
to be understood as to understand;
to be loved as to love;
For it is in giving that we receive;
It is in pardoning that we are pardoned;
It is in dying that we are born to eternal life.

From *Side by Side: Families Learning and Living the Faith Together*, by Delia Halverson. Copyright © 2002 by Abingdon Press. Reproduced by permission.

ANN B. DAVIS

You may know this woman by the name of "Schultze" (on the Bob Cummings Show in the 1950s on TV) or "Alice" (on the Brady Bunch in the 1970s). When Ms. Davis was 49 she "found something more fun than show business—loving the Lord and the whole church renewal experience." Since the late 1970s she has traveled around the country telling people about God and working in centers for the needy. She occasionally returns to Hollywood for television appearances. She explains her work with the needy, "When you love somebody, you want to make them happy. You do what the Lord wants you to do."

For many years the typical day of this gentle, wise, and funny woman included washing the socks of a homeless man at the St. Francis Center or bagging food and performing other chores for the needy at Central Denver Community Services. Barbara Roark, the center's executive director, said, "It means so much to the fellows for someone so well-known to do their dirty socks. She's no different from the other volunteers. She's just well-known."

Although Ann Davis has received two Emmy awards for her TV performances, she finds her real joy in caring for others.

CRAIG KIELBURGER

Young people, when met with the world's problems, sometimes think, "What can I do? I'm only a kid." The story of Craig Kielburger shows that kids can do a lot to solve problems and make the world a better place!

Craig was only 12-years-old when he read a newspaper article about a young child in Pakistan who had been sold into slavery by his family for a few dollars. After six years of work, the boy escaped from the slave-owner. Later, he was murdered because he took a stand against the practice of child labor. Craig was shocked to learn that children in some countries are forced into slavery. He and his young friends formed a group to discuss this problem. Led by Craig, this group dedicated themselves to the goal of helping children around the world who live in poverty and harsh conditions. They named their group Free the Children. From this simple beginning, Free the Children grew into a worldwide organization that continues its work in many different countries. They have help from older young people and adults, but they run the show. Their work includes raising money, and sponsoring projects to promote health care and education. Thousands of children are living greatly improved lives because of the work done by Free the Children. They also work to get the message out to the public about the needs of exploited children, and encourage others to participate in this important effort.

So, the next time you think there is nothing you can do to help others, remember Craig!

MARY MCLEOD BETHUNE

Mary McLeod Bethune was the first in her family to be born into freedom rather than slavery. The midwife who delivered her spoke a prophecy: "She will be different. She came with her eyes wide open. She'll see things before her time." At age nine she could pick 250 pounds of cotton a day, but she could not read or write.

Mary Tells Her Own Story

I used to pray every day. Please, God, let someone teach me to read and write. Well, I got my education and was determine to become a missionary in Africa. But my application came back saying, "no vacancies at that time for colored missionaries." It was the greatest disappointment in my life.

God refused to let me go to Africa. And in a little Methodist church where I learned to love God, I also learned that God often says no. By saying no to my dreams, God made me a missionary to all the people of all races of the United States.

With her savings of one dollar and fifty cents, Mary started a school for black girls in Daytona Beach, Florida. Today it has become the impressive institution called Bethune-Cookman College. People say it is a college built on prayer. And the little girl who could not read or write became an advisor to three U.S. presidents and was one of the best-known women in America.

It has been reported that she once said, "Walk bravely in the light. . . . Faith ought not to be a puny thing. If you believe, believe like a giant, and may God grant you not peace, but glory."[2]

2. "A Worker with God" from student leaflet of *Invitation: Bible Studies for Elementary C*, Graded Press, 1989.

From *Side by Side: Families Learning and Living the Faith Together*, by Delia Halverson. Copyright © 2002 by Abingdon Press. Reproduced by permission.

DR. BEN CARSON

When Dr. Ben Ben Carson was in the fifth grade in school, he decided, "I'm just dumb." Ben believed that he was dumb and that he would never amount to anything. But one day Ben Carson realized that he was not dumb and that God had plans for him to become a doctor and to help heal others.

Ben grew up in the inner city of Detroit, Michigan. At first he didn't care about school, and his grades showed it. But his mother began to tell Ben that he could and must do better in school.

By the time Ben was in middle school and high school, he had become an excellent student. He also went to church and Sunday school Ben prayed and prayed to God, asking what he should do. He believed that God wanted him to become a doctor.

Ben went to Yale College and to the University of Michigan Medical School. When he was 33, he became the director of pediatric neurosurgery at Johns Hopkins Hospital in Baltimore, Maryland.

Ben Carson has been called "gifted hands" because he has helped hundreds of dying children get a second chance at life. He has been on many television programs and in newspapers because he has helped in the healing of so many children. He performs rare brain operations. He has helped separate Siamese twins who were joined at the back of the head and has saved many other children who might not have lived.

Dr. Ben Carson is a Christian doctor. He prays before every operation. He believes that God helps him in all of the operations. Dr. Carson uses the talents and skills God has given him to help heal children.[1]

1. "Gifted Hands, Healing Hands" from *New Invitation: Grades 5-6, Student*—Winter 1996–97, page 6. Cokesbury, 1996.

From *Side by Side: Families Learning and Living the Faith Together*, by Delia Halverson. Copyright © 2002 by Abingdon Press. Reproduced by permission.

ANNIE DODGE WAUNEKA

Annie Dodge was born on an April day in 1910 in a hogan, which is a Navajo Indian house. Her home was round in shape and made of log walls covered with mud. There was a hole in the top of the roof to carry away the smoke from a fire in the center of a dirt floor.

Navajo children were expected to work. She rose every morning at sunrise and drove a flock of sheep and goats to a pasture in the foothills to graze. When Annie was eight years old, her father sent her to a government school. Many children in the school because ill with influenza. Since there was only one nurse, Annie helped by washing the children's faces with cool cloths and feeding them soup. She wanted to do something for the poor health of her people.

Annie grew into a lovely young woman, married, and had eight children, two of whom died. Although she was busy with her own children, she visited the hogans of her people and talked about the dirt floors and the need to keep things clean. She wanted her people to borrow ideas from others which would help, but she didn't want them to lose the good and beautiful in their way of life.

Through the years Annie was able to bring about many changes to improve the health of her people. In 1963 President Lyndon Johnson honored her as an outstanding citizen. He pinned the Freedom Award to her blouse. The Navajos named her "The Badge Woman."[3]

3. Adapted from "The Badge Woman," *Church & Home Leaflets*, July 3, 1983. Nashville: Graded Press, 1983.

BROTHER LAWRENCE

Three hundred years ago in France, there was a young man by the name of Lawrence. He thought that he was awkward and could not do anything to please God. Eventually, his faith led him to become a monk. Monks choose to give up ordinary jobs and not to marry or have families. They speak of themselves as brothers. Women who make this choice are called nuns and speak of themselves as sisters. Today many monks and nuns live in houses like everyone else, but 300 years ago monks and nuns lived in monasteries and convents.

Brother Lawrence followed all the rules and prayed as he was required to do. He was put to work in the kitchen as a cook, a kind of work he hated. But he began talking to God at any time, even in the kitchen and when he was walking in the halls. He would pray something as simple as, "Lord, I can't do this without your help." This brought him tremendous peace and joy. Many people, even the chief leader, began to ask him for his secret of combining work with prayer. He said he was "practicing the presence of God." He felt that prayer was simply the sense of the Presence of God, realizing that God is with you no matter where you are or what you are doing. He even wrote a little booklet with suggestions for this. The booklet has been published many times in the past 300 years. You can still buy it today. It is called *The Practice of the Presence of God*.

Friendship

Mobiles
Draw symbols or small pictures about friendship. Cut the symbols or pictures into varying shapes. Punch a hole at the top of each drawing. Make a mobile by attaching varying lengths of string to the hole in the drawing and tying them to a doweling. You may make several levels of dowling and drawings. Attach a string to the top of the mobile for hanging.

Crossword Hopscotch
Enjoy a game of hopscotch. As you hop in and out of the game, you will stand on only one foot. After you pick up the stone you may stand on two feet to turn around. Throw the stone into the second square. Then hop in the first square and then into the second square and pick up the stone, turn around, and hop out. Everyone in the group says the word that is printed on the square each time someone hops into it. Each person takes a turn. Then you throw the stone to the next square and continue until everyone has finished, or until you are ready to move on to the next center. If you have young children in your group, make exceptions for their ability.

Write a friend
Choose a piece of note paper and write a letter to a friend. Tell the friend about your study on friendship and anything else you'd like to share. Place the letter in an envelope and write the friend's name on the front. When you get home, address and stamp the envelope and mail it.

Make a Friendship Banner
Using the materials provided at the center, create a banner about friendship with pictures and words. You may use sayings such as: "Friendship is one large milkshake with two straws." "Friendship is an evergreen tree." "Friendship is a bicycle for two."

Make a Collage
Find pictures that tell about friends or friendship in the magazines and cut them out and glue them to the collage poster.

Make Bumper Stickers

Create bumper stickers by writing some of the following scriptures on the strips of paper. You may draw pictures or symbols to illustrate them. Proverbs 10:12; 11:13; 15:13*a*; 15:30; 17:17*a*; 18:24*b*; 24:26; 25:11; 27:6.

Read Bible Stories

Read aloud (or tell in your own words) these Bible stories. Then discuss the positive or negative aspects of each. What actions were those of friends?
Cain and Abel: Genesis 4
Abram and Lot: Genesis 12, 13
Jonathan and David: 1 Samuel 20
Ruth and Naomi: Book of Ruth
Jesus and Lazarus: John 11:1-44; 12:1-11

Cycle of Friendship

Using a pencil or crayon and a large sheet of paper, draw a picture of your friendship with a specific person. Use straight lines, circles, spirals, stair-steps, and other symbols. Be sure to include both the "ups and downs" of the friendship. Share your drawing with others in your family/group.

Build a Neighborhood

Using the blocks and figures provided, create a neighborhood. Be sure to include school, church, your home, homes of friends, and stores.
    Pretend that you are traveling through the neighborhood to a friend's house.

Paint a Friendship Picture

Use the paints provided and paint a picture of friendship. This may include people, symbols, and words.

Paraphrase Scripture

Read 1 Corinthians 13 and write what it says in your own words.

Act as Reporter

Make a name tag that says "Press" and put it on. Using the recorder, interview someone in your group about a friend that he or she has and what makes their friendship special.

Take a Picture

Use the camera to take a picture of your family/group. Write the names of the friends in the picture on the back of the picture.

Crosses

The cross is the primary symbol of our Christian faith. We use the cross to remind us of the way that Jesus died for us. Some people use the sign of the cross when they pray, remembering that Jesus said to "take up your cross and follow me." This may be a small sign on the forehead or a larger sign, from forehead to breast, then left to right.

Some crosses are ornate and some are plain. Some churches use a cross with the body of Christ attached to it. Protestant churches usually use an empty cross, remembering the resurrection. There is a variety of crosses in use today, in fact more than 50 are found in Christian art. We will review a few.

Latin Cross
This is the most popular cross. It is the style that the Romans used to execute criminals, and is more likely the type of cross that was used to kill Jesus. Many churches are built in the form of a cross. This form is called a cruciform plan. The altar and pulpit are in the area above the "arms" of the cross, and people are seated in the lower part (nave) of the church and the arms (transcepts).

Celtic Cross
This is a variation of the Latin cross that was used by the Celts, an ancient people of the British Isles. This combines the Latin cross with the circle, which stands for eternal life. This cross is popular in cemeteries because we remember that although the person's body has died we believe the soul of the person has eternal life.

Anchor Cross
Another old style of cross combines the anchor and the cross. Sometimes this sign is combined with the symbol of the fish. When the first century Christians had to worship in secret, they used underground passageways called the catacombs. The anchor cross was carved in the walls of those catacombs. People who did not know about Christianity would think it was only an anchor, but the

Christian would know to return to that spot to worship in secret. In Hebrews 6:19 hope is described as a "sure and steadfast anchor of the soul." We have hope because Jesus came, and the early Christians needed a reminder of that hope during their persecution.

St. Andrew's Cross
The name of this cross comes from the tradition that says that St. Andrew (one of Jesus' disciples) was martyred (put to death) on this form of cross.

Greek Cross
This simple form of cross is distinguished by its four equal arms. Some people use the symbolism four to represent the four Gospels.

Maltese Cross
This is a form of the Greek cross developed when European pilgrims traveled to Jerusalem during the eleventh century. Concerned laymen organized the Knights of St. John to protect the pilgrims, and the people of Malta allowed the knights to use their island as headquarters. The cross appears to be four spearheads meeting in the center. The eight outer points stand for the eight Beatitudes in Matthew 5:3-11.

Jerusalem (Pilgrim's) Cross
Another cross from the eleventh century pilgrims is the Jerusalem cross. This cross added four small crosses to the Greek cross. The five crosses in total reminds us of the five wounds that Jesus suffered when he was crucified.

Cross of Triumph
Combining the cross with the globe of the world is called the cross of triumph, symbolizing how the message of Christ has spread all over the world. When we look at it we can remember the Christian schools in India, a new clinic in Panama, and a new church building for a very old congregation in Mozambique. From east to west and from north to south, the gospel has spread.

From *Side by Side: Families Learning and Living the Faith Together,* by Delia Halverson. Copyright © 2002 by Abingdon Press. Reproduced by permission.

A Lenten Palm Calendar

Lent is a time to prepare for Easter. It is a time when we remember what Jesus taught us about God. The readings and activity suggestions will guide you through Lent.

Using a strip of green construction paper, make a long "stem" to attach the palm fronds on. On Sundays, read the scripture reading and each weekday select one of the activities for that week. When you have read the scripture or done the activity, fasten it to the stem of the palm branch with tape or glue. Keep the palm branch in an obvious place to remind you of Lent.

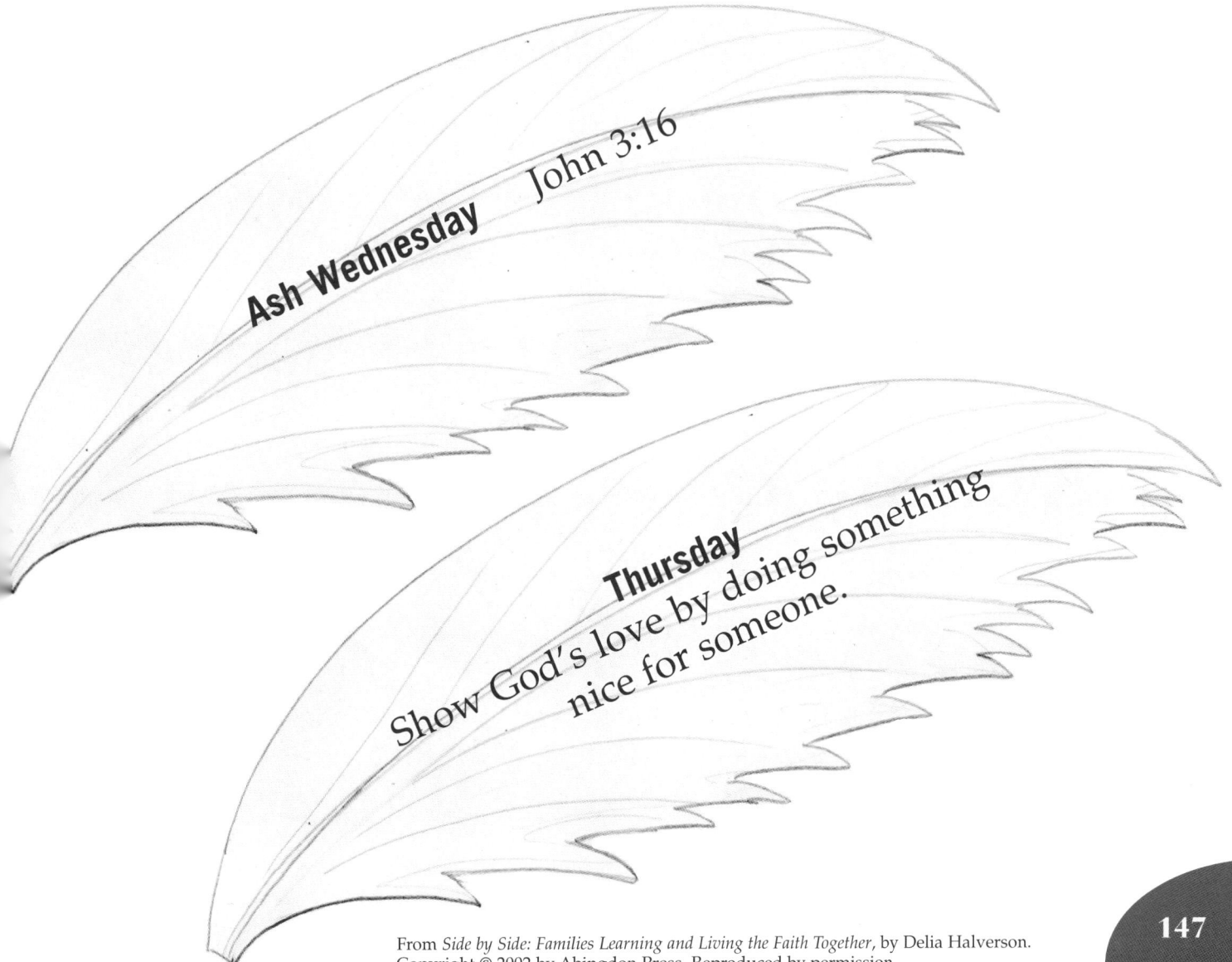

Ash Wednesday   John 3:16

Thursday
Show God's love by doing something nice for someone.

Hosanna
Hosanna
Hosanna
Hosanna
Hosanna

Friday
Pray the Lord's Prayer

Saturday
Jog, walk, or ride a bike and enjoy the
wind in your hair.

1st Sunday   John 8:12
*Count the number of light switches you have in your house and pray for
families who have no electricity. Remember that Christ brought a different type of light.*

Go outdoors at different hours on a sunny day and look at your shadow. Notice how the
shadow changes as the sun is at a different position in the sky.

*Find a window where the sun is shining in. Put an article of clothing in the sunshine for 30 minutes or more and then
put it on. How does the warmth of the clothing remind you of God's love?*

Eat by candlelight with the other lights turned out. At the end of the meal, blow out the candle and sit in the
darkness for two minutes.

Make a sunshine picture, perhaps of a sunrise or a sunset.

Light a candle at supper and talk about Jesus.

2nd Sunday   Read 1 John 4:7-8.
Help with jobs around the house.

Do something nice for someone but don't let them know who did it.

Write a letter to someone telling them that God loves them and you do too.

Visit a friend who is sick or someone who is in a nursing home.

"Adopt" a grandparent and share your love with an older person.

Research hunger. Go to the library or go to www.thehungersite.com or www.churchworldservice.org or play this
hunger game http://www.churchworldservice.org/decisions/index.htm on the Internet.

3rd Sunday — Matthew 21:22

Say the blessing at dinner.

Lead a family devotion.

Pray for your church today.

Find a Psalm that you like in the Bible and share it with your family.

Make a list of all that you are thankful for and pray a prayer of thanks.

Pray for world peace.

4th Sunday — Ezekiel 36:26

Write a poem about Easter.

Smell a flower and look for new life.

Take time after supper to tell the story of Easter. One person begins the story and stops at one point. Then someone else carry the story on, taking turns until the story is finished.

Enjoy a special meal, like Jesus enjoyed a meal with his friends.

Think of one new thing you have done during Lent that you will continue to do after Easter.

Prepare your house and make it fresh for Easter.

Easter — *Matthew 28:19-20*

Pentecost Symbols

Wind
The wind is a translation for the Greek word *spirit*. Acts 2 refers to the wind at the first Christian Pentecost when the Holy Spirit came to the disciples.

Three Circles
This symbol shows one of the many ways to represent the Trinity: *God the Father, the Son,* and *the Holy Spirit.* At Pentecost, when the Holy Spirit came, the Trinity was completed.

Flame
In the story of Pentecost (Acts 2) when the apostles were filled with the Holy Spirit, reference is made to tongues of fire. Fire symbolizes what God does through the Holy Spirit.

Fish

The fish was a secret code during the early church. When pagans painted a fish on a home it meant that a funeral banquet was to be held. Christians adopted the symbol as a signal that a service was to be held there that night, thereby fooling the pagans.

The fish was worn and used as a sign of identification. It was used by the persecuted Christians to convey a message to other Christians without the message being understood by the pagans. While talking to someone a Christian would draw half of a fish in the sand with the foot. If the other person was a Christian he or she would finish the symbol. The first initials of the phrase "Jesus Christ, Son of God, Savior" spell the word "fish" in Greek.

Torch

The torch was used for light in the early services when Christians met in the catacombs. It later represented Christ, the light of the world. Today our acolytes carry the light (representing Christ) into the sanctuary and back out, signifying our taking the light (Christ) into the world.

Monograms

Monograms were popular in the early church. X (chi) and P (rho) are two Greek letters. When combined, the letters represent church—the symbol of hope.[1]

1. "Celebrate an Anniversary," by Delia Halverson. *Fellowship Times*, Summer 1981, pages 3-4, Graded Press.

Symbols of Our Faith

Candle
*symbolizes
Christ as
the light of
the world.*
Luke
2:21-32;
John
1:1-9;
8:12;
12:44-46;
and
1 John
1:5-7

Dove *symbolizes the Holy Spirit (God within us).*
Mark 1:9-11; John 14:25-27;
Matthew 28:16-20

Empty cross
*symbolizes
Christ dying
for us and his
power over
death.*
John
19:16–20:18

Flame
*symbolizes the
Holy Spirit at
Pentecost.*
Acts 2:1-21

Bread and Chalice
*symbolize the bread and wine that Jesus had with
his disciples at the Last
Supper.*
Matthew 26:26-30;
Mark 14:22-26;
Luke 22:14-20;
1 Corinthians 11:23-26

Star
*symbolizes
the birth of Jesus
into the world.*
Matthew 2:1-12

Rainbow
symbolizes our covenant with God.
Genesis 9:8-17; Exodus 34:27-28; Luke 22:14-20

Fish
*symbolizes Jesus' command to be fishers of people.
Used as secret symbol in early church.*
Matthew 4:18-22; Mark 1:14-20; John 6:1-13

COLORS OF THE CHURCH YEAR

Purple is the color of both penitence (regretful) and royalty. It symbolizes our sorrow for wrongs and our belief that God, through the coming of Christ, is the supreme royalty over us. Purple is used during Advent and Lent. Advent is the time that we prepare for the celebration of Jesus' birth (royalty), and Lent is the time we prepare (penitence) for his death and celebration of his Resurrection.

White symbolizes festive joy and celebration. We use white for Christmas and Easter, as well as special occasions in the church, such as a wedding or when we have Communion and remember Jesus.

Green is a color of growth and is used in the seasons of ordinary (ordered) time after Epiphany and Pentecost. It is a time when we remember how the early church grew and spread the good news of Christ to others throughout the world. It is a time of sharing with others.

Red is the color of fire. It tells us that our faith became like fire on the Day of Pentecost two thousand years ago and comes alive for us today. Red symbolizes the Holy Spirit that lives within us. It is used at Pentecost and sometimes for several Sundays afterward. We may *also* use it for special days.

BOOKS OF THE BIBLE

To be used with the session on "Bible" on p. 83.

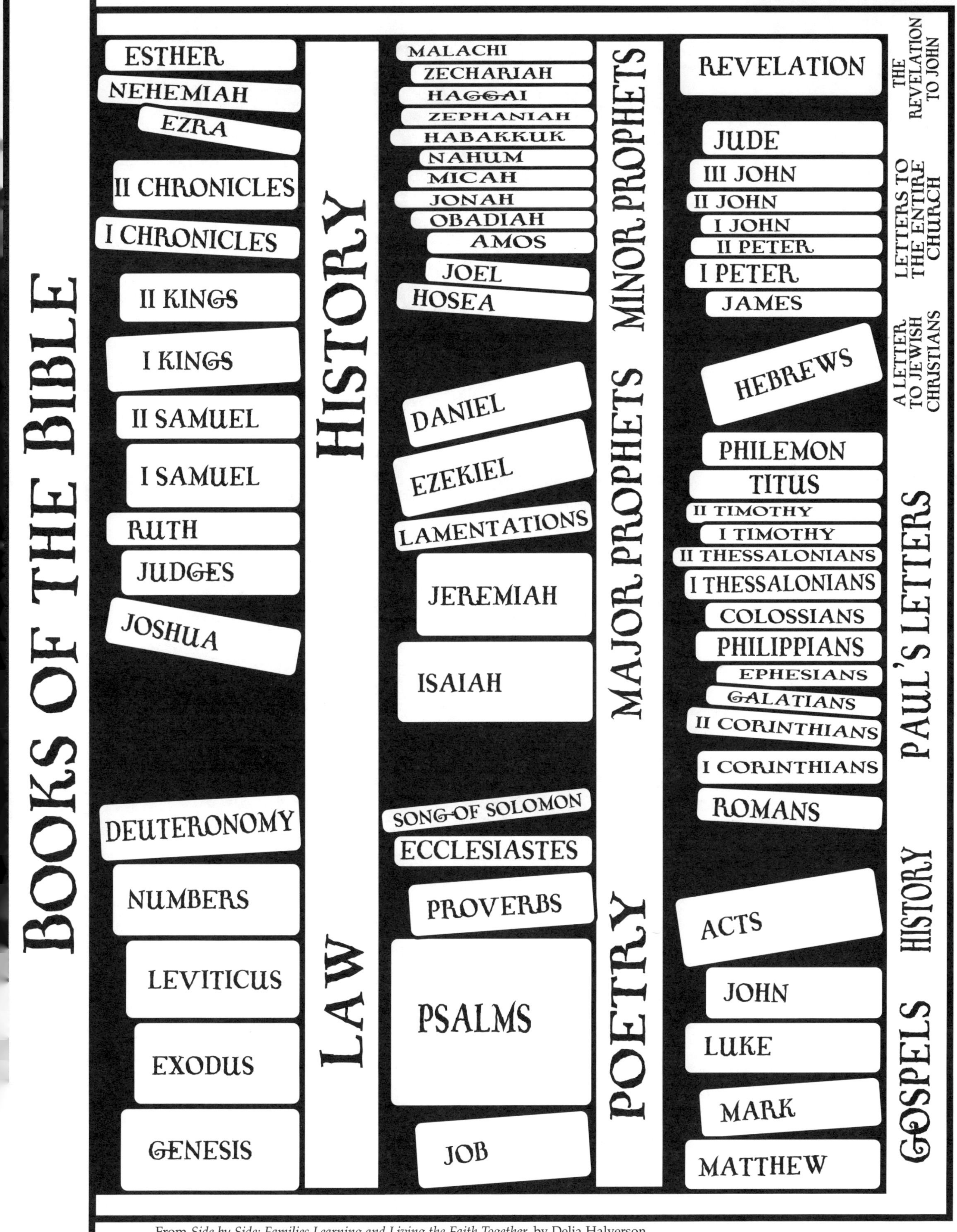

HISTORY

ESTHER
NEHEMIAH
EZRA
II CHRONICLES
I CHRONICLES
II KINGS
I KINGS
II SAMUEL
I SAMUEL
RUTH
JUDGES
JOSHUA

LAW

DEUTERONOMY
NUMBERS
LEVITICUS
EXODUS
GENESIS

MINOR PROPHETS

MALACHI
ZECHARIAH
HAGGAI
ZEPHANIAH
HABAKKUK
NAHUM
MICAH
JONAH
OBADIAH
AMOS
JOEL
HOSEA

MAJOR PROPHETS

DANIEL
EZEKIEL
LAMENTATIONS
JEREMIAH
ISAIAH

POETRY

SONG OF SOLOMON
ECCLESIASTES
PROVERBS
PSALMS
JOB

REVELATION
THE REVELATION TO JOHN

LETTERS TO THE ENTIRE CHURCH

JUDE
III JOHN
II JOHN
I JOHN
II PETER
I PETER
JAMES

A LETTER TO JEWISH CHRISTIANS

HEBREWS

PAUL'S LETTERS

PHILEMON
TITUS
II TIMOTHY
I TIMOTHY
II THESSALONIANS
I THESSALONIANS
COLOSSIANS
PHILIPPIANS
EPHESIANS
GALATIANS
II CORINTHIANS
I CORINTHIANS
ROMANS

HISTORY

ACTS

GOSPELS

JOHN
LUKE
MARK
MATTHEW

From *Side by Side: Families Learning and Living the Faith Together,* by Delia Halverson.
Copyright © 2002 by Abingdon Press. Reproduced by permission.

From *Side by Side: Families Learning and Living the Faith Together*, by Delia Halverson. Copyright © 2002 by Abingdon Press. Reproduced by permission.

Learning About Bible References

Handout 12
TO BE USED WITH THE SESSION "BIBLE," ON PAGE 83.

1. **Books:** Look in the Table of Contents at the Old Testament books. Find the book named Joshua. Find the page number on the list and turn to that page in your Bible. The name of the book will be at the beginning, and some Bibles will have information about the book, such as what the book contains, who is believed to have written it, when it was believed to have been written, and what the circumstances were at that time. Look over this information.

2. **Chapters:** The chapters and verses were not added to the books of the Bible until hundreds of years after Jesus lived. They help us to find the exact location of what we want to study. Look at the chapter numbers in the book of Joshua. They are the large numbers.

   In the Bible reference, the name of the book is the first thing listed. We've found the book of Joshua. Next to the book name in the reference is a number. This is the chapter number. We want to find chapter 24. Find that now in your groups.

3. **Verse:** The chapters are divided into verses. The number after the colon is the verse. If there is more than one verse, it will be indicated with a dash between the first and last verses in the reference, or by commas if the verses do not immediately follow each other. In your groups, find Joshua 24:15. (Or the book of Joshua, the 24th chapter, and the 15th verse.)

4. **Part of a verse:** Sometimes we only want to read a part of the verse. This is indicated by using a, b, or c. If it lists "a," you read only the first part; "b" means you read the second; and "c" means you read only the third part. Find Joshua 24:15*b* and *c*; and read it in your group.

Hebrew Alphabet Code

The Hebrew language is very old. Hebrew was the language of Old Testament people. Hebrew was the language of Hosea and the other prophets.

The Hebrew alphabet is still used today by Jewish people all over the world. Use the Hebrew alphabet code on the bottom of this page to work the following puzzle. You will find some words that the prophet Hosea spoke for God.

What we now know as the Bible began thousands of years ago as stories around campfires. The Hebrew tribes of Israel first began writing the stories down about 1100 B.C. It was not all written at one time, but over a period of many, many years by many people. We have no idea who actually wrote much of the Bible, but we have some pretty good guesses.

The Old Testament has scriptures that Jesus knew and used when he was alive on this earth. However the decision of the exact books to be officially included in the Hebrew scriptures was not made until the end of the first century after Jesus' death. These scriptures are still used by the Jewish community, or the Hebrews, of today.

The New Testament was written after the death of Jesus. It is about the life of Jesus, about the early church, and contains letters written to early church congregations and people in the early church. At first there were many accounts of Jesus' life being circulated, and by the second century after his death the leaders agreed on the four Gospels we have today. It was during the fourth century, over four hundred years after Jesus, that the church leaders finally decided exactly which other writings should be officially a part of our Bible.

Translations

The Bible was not originally written in English. The New Testament was written in Greek, and it had no spaces and no punctuation. Try reading the following verse from the Bible in the Greek fashion:

AGAINJESUSSPOKETOTHEMSAYINGIAMTHELIGHTOFTHE-
WORLDWHOEVERFOLLOWSMEWILLNEVERWALKINDARK-
NESSBUTWILLHAVETHELIGHTOFLIFE

If you have difficulty reading it, turn to John 8:12 in the New Revised Standard Version.

The Old Testament was written in Hebrew and also did not have punctuation or spaces. It also did not have vowels. Try reading the following verse in Hebrew fashion:

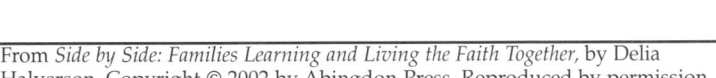

THLRDSMSHPHRDSHLLNTWNT

If you have difficulty reading this, turn to Psalm 23:1.

When the mechanical printing press was finally invented by Johann Gutenberg in Germany, the first book to be printed was the Bible in 1456. This made the Bible more accessible to more people. William Tyndale stated that "A boy who drives the plough in England shall know more of the Bible than many priests" when he translated it into English in 1525. Since then there have been many English translations.

A true translation of the Bible goes back to the earliest known manuscripts which are in Hebrew and Greek and also studies other writing of the era, taking into consideration what life was like at the time the verses were written. We need new translations regularly because the meanings of our own words change over the years. When the King James Version was translated, the people spoke English in the manner of Shakespeare's time. Then the words "thee" and "thou" were used only for friends and family members. In formal and legal settings, they used "you" and "your." Now we have reversed this use, and so if we see God as a personal God, we should use "you" and "your" today instead of "thee" and "thou."

Translate the following verses, using "you" and "your" instead of "thee" and "thou." You may also want to change some of the endings of some words (such as preparest and anointest) to a more modern English, and use "Even" instead of "Yea."

Yea, though, I walk through the valley of the shadow of death, I will fear no evil: for thou art with me; thy rod and thy staff they comfort me. Thou preparest a table before me in the presence of mine enemies: thou anointest my head with oil; my cup runneth over. Psalm 23:4-5, King James Version

Paraphrases

When a person paraphrases the Bible, he or she takes the idea of the text and uses his or her own words to restate the meaning. Here is a paraphrase of the same verses.

Even though I have many times of struggle, I am not afraid because I know that you, God, are with me. You give me comfort and guidance. You help me, even when I face my enemies. You let me know that I am special. You fill me with your love.

Try writing a paraphrase for one of these scripture references:

Genesis 1:21	Isaiah 12:2
Genesis 8:22	Matthew 6:31-32
Psalm 19:1	Ephesians 4:32
Psalm 118:24	

Hidden Bible Book Names

Can you find 15 books of the Bible in the following paragraph? Underline them. The first one is underlined for you, and there are 14 others.

Here are some re<u>mark</u>s about the Bible. Numbers of the readers will have the revelation of the truth about the Bible. The stories were first told around campfires and in the homes. Sometimes they used walls of caves or clay tablets to write on. Then they were written on the skins of animals and later on a fiber made from plants. These skins and pounded fiber were rolled into scrolls for easy carrying. Yes, there were real books later, but then they had to be copied by hand. This was usually done by a monk. He brews over the manuscript, looking so hard at his work. Mistakes could easily happen. You can judge so for yourself. The monks who copied the scriptures would probably admit it usually resulted in loud lamentations when they worked long hours.

Sometimes the job of translating the Bible puts the translators in a jam, especially when the word in one language does not have an exact meaning in another. But some people find it a most fascinating puzzle. This work is a real lulu, keeping the translators looking so hard for facts.

Note: The key to finding these is in the leader's instructions for this session.

Getting into the Bible

We can use the Bible as a tool in our faith journey if we spend some time becoming familiar with its content and the way that it is set up. The following exercise will help you to find the sections of the Bible. As you learn which books are in which section, you will be able to locate passages with ease.

GETTING STARTED

Turn to the table of contents in your Bible. The Bible is made up of various sections or books. It is like a mini-library, all bound together in one volume. In fact, the word *Bible* means *books*. If at any time you have difficulty in finding a passage quickly, feel free to turn to the table of contents. You might want to place a marker there so that you can find it easily.

The way that a Bible reference is written helps us to locate it. For example, when we write John 3:16, we know that the reference is in the book of John, in the third chapter and the sixteenth verse. If we are concentrating on only part of a verse, then we may use "a" or "b" after the verse number, such as Matthew 10:5*b*. When the reference is for more than one verse (Luke 2:1-20), we write it with a hyphen, indicating that we are looking for verses one through twenty. If we want selected verses in the same chapter that do not follow one another, we use commas between them (Psalm 8:1, 3). If the passage continues into the next chapter, we use the word through (Matthew 1:18 through 2:12). If we are looking for sections of verses in the same book but in different chapters, we use a semicolon, such as these stories of Jesus' healing ministry: Luke 17:11-19; 18:35-43.

OLD AND NEW TESTAMENTS

The books of the Bible are divided into two sections, the Old Testament, which was written before Jesus' birth (in the front of the Bible) and the New Testament, which was written after Jesus' death (in the back of the Bible).

Using the table of contents, locate the beginning of the New Testament and then turn to it. Mark this place with your finger and close the book. Look at the edge of the Bible and discover that there are more pages in the Old Testament than in the New Testament. The Old Testament covers many more years than the New Testament.

BOOKS OF WISDOM

Take your finger out of the Bible and reopen the book to the middle. You will probably find the Psalms. This book is found in the center of the Bible and is generally referred to as wisdom literature. The wisdom books include Job through Solomon (or the Song of Songs).

CREATION AND LAW

With the Bible still opened to the middle, divide the front half in half again. You will probably find yourself near the end of the book of Deuteronomy. The books in your left hand will include books that tell us about creation and the law that the Jewish people of Jesus' day lived by. These books also include the stories of people who lived long ago, before Israel became a nation.

OLD TESTAMENT HISTORY

The books in your right hand will include books of the Old Testament history (Joshua through Esther). These come between the books of creation and law and the wisdom books. They tell of the rulers of Israel and the trials and problems that they had as they fought with other nations and among themselves.

PROPHETS

The remaining books in the Old Testament (following the wisdom books) are books of the prophets (Isaiah through Malachi). Prophets are persons who spoke to the people for God, and there were many of these during Old Testament times. They are divided into what we call the major and minor prophets. They are called this not because of their importance, but because of the size of each book. The major prophets are larger books and are in the front; the minor prophets have fewer pages and are the last books of the Old Testament.

NEW TESTAMENT HISTORY (GOSPELS AND ACTS)

Close the Bible now and open it again in the center. Divide the back half in half again (the pages in your right hand). You will find that you are near the beginning of the New Testament (Matthew).

Holding only the pages of the New Testament, divide this section in half. The New Testament also has two parts. The pages in your left hand can be called the history part of the New Testament. This includes the four Gospels which tell us about Jesus' life and teachings (Matthew, Mark, Luke, and John). We call these the Gospels (or good news) because they tell of the good news of Jesus' coming. This first

From *Side by Side: Families Learning and Living the Faith Together,* by Delia Halverson. Copyright © 2002 by Abingdon Press. Reproduced by permission.

half of the New Testament also includes Acts, which is a book that tells about the early church after Jesus died.

THE LETTERS

The remaining part of the New Testament (the pages in your right hand) is primarily made up of letters written to the people of some of the first churches. Some of these letters have the names of the people to whom they are written as the titles; others have the names of the persons whom we believe to have been the writers.

REVELATION

Turn to the last book in the Bible, Revelation. It is the only apocalyptic book in the New Testament. This is a type of writing that was popular in the last centuries before Christ, when everyone was discouraged and waiting for the Messiah. Daniel is an apocalyptic book in the Old Testament, but most of the apocalyptic books of that time were not included in the Bible.

Revelation was written during a time when the Christians who refused to worship the Roman emperor were placed in prisons and killed. Apocalyptic writing uses a lot of symbols and imagery. People today have many different views about the meanings of the symbols in this book. Although the true meanings of the author may be lost, we do know that he was trying to tell the people that although things may have seemed very bad for them, God would win out in the end.

From *Side by Side: Families Learning and Living the Faith Together*, by Delia Halverson. Copyright © 2002 by Abingdon Press. Reproduced by permission.

Plan a Devotion

POSSIBLE THEMES AND SCRIPTURE:

Showing God's love   Luke 19:1-10 *(Zacchaeus)*

We are all loved by God   Romans 12:3-8
                                   (We are all one body)

Importance of saying "Thank you"   Luke 17:11-19
                                   (One of ten lepers tells Jesus thanks)

Friends care for each other   Mark 2:1-12
                                   (Friends bring man to Jesus)

Jesus teaches about prayer   Matthew 6:7-15
                                   (Lord's Prayer)

We share the story of Jesus   Acts 8:26-40
                                   (Philip tells of Jesus)

Knowing Jesus causes us to change Acts 16:16-40
                                   (Jailer turns about)

We help in the church   1 Samuel 2:18
                                   (Samuel helps Eli)

We share what we have   John 6:1-14
                                   (A boy shares his lunch)

God forgives us   Luke 15:11-32
                                   (Parable of forgiving father)

God cares for each one   Luke 15:3-7
                                   (Jesus' story of lost sheep)

We must love everyone   Luke 10:25-37
                                   (Parable of good Samaritan)

God made the world   Genesis 1:1, 27, 31 *(Creation)*

Jesus loves the children   Luke 18:15-17
                                   (Jesus and children)

God has a plan for us   1 Samuel 3:1-10, 19-20
                                   (God calls Samuel)

Theme: _____

Scripture: _____

Feeling into activity/conversation *(an activity or conversation that helps us feel the emotions of the persons in the story):* _____

_____

_____

_____

Meet with Scripture *(telling the story or an activity that makes you feel as if you are there):* _____

_____

_____

_____

Respond-out-of activity/conversation *(something that you can do or talk about, such as a project, a way of sharing the story, or a change in action or attitude):* _____

_____

_____

_____

Prayer: _____

_____

_____

_____

_____

_____

Water Facts

- No life on earth is possible without water.
- Water provides a home for nearly 90% of all living plants.
- Water covers 75% of the earth's surface, but 99% of the water is either salt water in the oceans or frozen in glaciers.
- If all the glacier ice that exists today melted, a layer of water approximately 196 feet deep would be added to all of the world's oceans—and many coastal lands would be submerged.
- You can live without food for more than a month, but without water for less than a week.
- Every day 1 billion people on earth drink contaminated water.
- 25,000 people die every day for lack of clean drinking water.
- About 80% of all sickness and disease can be attributed to inadequate water or sanitation.
- Although only a fifth of a gallon is all one needs to survive, a person must take in 2 1/2 quarts of water a day to maintain a normal water balance in the body.
- Mothers in some countries walk 15 miles each day for water, sometimes requiring 8 hours a day. In the U.S., on the average, we use 200 gallons of water a day per person.

It takes water to make things:
- One Sunday newspaper takes about 150 gallons
- One automobile tire takes about 2,000 gallons
- One slice of bread takes about 37 gallons
- One ton of oil takes about 180 tons of water
- One ton of paper takes about 250 tons of water
- One ton of steel takes about 150 tons of water
- One ton of grain takes about 1,000 tons of water

Source: "Drink from the Well of Living Water" by Alternatives for Simple Living.
1-800-821-6153 www.simpleliving.org
Used by permission.